HANDLING THE CEO

MIRELA HOLT

This book is dedicated to all who need a four-letter word (or more than one) and the thought of a good smutty book waiting for them at home to get them through the day.

So please, if swearing and open door sex scenes are too much for you, stop here.

That being said, be mindful this book also mentions drug usage, body image issues/body shaming, racial insults, minor instances of violence including against teenagers, death of spouse/parent. Alcohol usage is also present in the book.

You can relax, this is not a dark romance so the triggers listed are not overwhelming the book, but I don't want you all reading something you would be uncomfortable with.

XO,
Mirela

JON

"J on, I have the best of news!" my Vice President enthusiastically yells over the line, so loud I have to pull my phone away from my head to keep my eardrum intact.

"What is it, Mike? Have we got the tire guys back?" I ask hopefully as I attempt to return to the office, still surprised my assistant somehow forgot to send the car over to my lawyer's place.

The day was nowhere near ending, but my patience was well past its finish line by midday. First, a supplier backed away from a productive tire deal at the last minute. Then, my ex-girlfriend decided she wanted me back and started texting me non-stop.

My favorite watch went on a fritz after banging it against my desk. To make matters worse, I now found myself walking back to my office instead of getting picked up by my driver.

The weather in Kerrington is what you'd expect for a town on Florida's Atlantic coast in February—not as humid as other times of the year but sunny and mild. The streets downtown are full of people for a Monday midday. I'm repeatedly bumped by someone, having to balance my coffee as I struggle to hold my phone.

"No silly, I got something even better—Dahlia Jara is back on the market!" One could see the exclamation marks in my VP's voice, and I imagined her doing a happy dance in her office chair. For a mother of three with 5 years until retirement, Michaela Jones—or Mike—often sounds like a teenager with some high school gossip she was just dying to tell everyone. Including me, unfortunately.

"Who?"

"Jeez—for someone who knows anyone who's anyone in aerospace, you'd think that you would know the name of the creator of Hove. She is a top-notch programmer, probably best in the business," she comments in a 'disappointed schoolteacher' tone.

I almost trip over myself, my coffee dangerously close to spilling over the delivery guy in front of me. Hove, the best route calculator in the industry, saves an airline company millions of dollars! Even better, hiring her would be a big 'fuck you very much' to my rival, Lex Aviation, and their cunt of a CEO, Miranda Lexington. Our two private jet manufacturing businesses have been in competition for years, but only recently my suppliers have been targeted.

Mike continues cheerfully, "She divorced her husband and doesn't want to work in the same company with him, so she is moving back here to Florida. I'll get a meeting set up between you two for next Tuesday. Try not to mess it up."

"That sounds great. And yes, as CEO with five thousand employees, I will attempt not to fuck up a basic interview with a programmer. Now, can you maybe hire me a new assistant also? Anya forgot to send the car over for me and I am walking back to the office." My VP handles all the contract work, but even with my focusing on engineering and production, having an executive assistant who isn't a complete moron is necessary.

"You? Walking?" she laughs like it's the funniest thing to ever happen. "Well, try not to break something vital. I must also remind you, you have lunch with the new tire suppliers at Giorgio's, so maybe you should just walk that way instead. Shall I drive there to ensure one of us is there?"

"Shit—I didn't get a notification on my phone! Anya really needs to go, Mike. If I walk to the office now, I won't make the restaurant! Fuck, I'm heading towards the meeting now. But would appreciate it if you were my back-up—just in case I don't make it," I grumble, ending the call.

However, fate had other thoughts. I turned right abruptly, just as the delivery guy turned left with a giant parcel. It forced me to step towards the curve to avoid him, directly into a light post and I spill my coffee all over my shirt.

Fuck, fuck again—now I have to stop and get a fresh shirt! Can't show up to a meeting with a new supplier with stains all over me. I run my fingers through my hair and ponder what the hell I am going to do. There is definitely not enough time to get back to either the office or home.

I have to find something around here.

But before I can locate a store, my phone rings again, and despite my shitty day so far, I don't even blink before picking that call up.

"Hey Jon, how are you?" My sister's voice makes my lips tug into a smile.

"Hey Tae," I answer breathlessly, trying to escape the crowd of people. "Is everything OK?"

"Uh yeah, I'm OK. I was just seeing how you were. My mom is at work again." She sounds dejected, another one to blame Miranda for. Normally I would let her tell me about her day, but time is ticking away and I need to get a move on.

"I am sorry, can't really talk a lot right now. Is it OK if I call you back tonight? I am a bit behind schedule."

"Oh, sure. Talk later." She cuts the call, and my heart breaks a bit. I vow to go see her soon, but for now I need to get to my meeting.

A quick google search shows an impressively rated men's clothes shop just around the corner, so I have to take my chances in finding something there.

As I make my way there with no more mishaps, I almost pass it by. The store seems quite unassuming from the front, just one suit on a mannequin in the window—no brand, just a dark green painted door. But even from the outside, I appreciate the great tailoring and material of the navy three-piece on display. Maybe my day is turning around, though so far it was still touch and go.

4

I step inside, glazing over several shelves and racks with men's suits, trousers, and shirts in a cozy yet elegant store, with dark wood paneling and green velvet chaises, but with strategic lighting on a few suits on display. Just as the suit outside, I could clearly see these giving my branded ones a run for their money. There is even a bar in a corner, with expensive bottles of whiskey and scotch on the shelf behind it. Very nice—more like something you would find in London rather than in Florida.

I spot a brunette by the tills, sitting on a bar chair, intensely typing on her phone with her back to me. She is dressed in ratty trainers, baggy khaki shorts with giant pockets on the sides, and a 'Hoe's before bros' t-shirt. She appears completely at odds with what I would expect of be a high-end men's clothes stores assistant.

"Excuse me," I start yet the little brat just raises a finger at me like her phone is much more important than a customer. "One minute," she answers in a muffled voice without turning, her leg twitching.

One minute I do not have as I stare at my watch. I now only have 40 minutes to get to the restaurant. Though looking at the girl she seems not to have a worry in the world—definitely not any worries about her job today. That ass, however, looks pretty good sitting perched on a highchair, and a trim waist gives her a delicious hourglass figure.

But I am done with the ones straight out of college after Sienna, so I need to stop ogling her behind. It's difficult to find anything in common with someone fifteen years younger. Physical attraction can only go so far, and I am tiring of simply finding bed partners with nothing to spark my interest beyond a romp in the sheets. If I am honest, despite my ex's supermodel appearance, I barely remember the sex, just some exaggerated moans from her and a warm body in my bed.

"Excuse me," I say again more forcefully, while rapping my fingers on the counter anxiously. "Perhaps Candy Crush can wait a bit until you can serve your customer if it wouldn't be too much trouble."

That stops her typing and she slowly turns in her chair and lifts her head towards me. The fire in her brown eyes makes me stop breathing as the girl—no, woman, as she is older than her outfit would indicate—exhales and starts smirking at me like I am about to be obliterated on the spot. Her dark hair is in a high ponytail, but the length of it is resting on one of her shoulders, and the bronze skin of her long and elegant neck is visible on the other side.

High cheekbones, long eyelashes, and soft pink lips—lower one slightly fuller than the top—and not a hint of makeup on her, complete what may be one of the most beautiful faces I have ever seen. And somehow, the fury-lasers her eyes are aiming at me from behind large glasses with black rims make my cock harden.

"Ah, if it isn't 'customer number one'." Her throaty sex voice shocks me even more. "Whatever shall I help you with? Maybe some patience—we have some on sale?"

"I... ahem... need a shirt ASAP." I ignore the jab as I struggle to formulate words when I gaze down and spot a pair of amazing tits straining her top, but I pivot my eyes back to her.

"Mm, in a hurry, are we? I most definitely should not waste a minute helping you then," she continues with the smirk on full blast.

"I need a shirt and I see you have plenty here—anyone else in the store who can help? Maybe someone who doesn't use the royal 'we' or should be way past dressing like Avril Lavigne?"

That makes her eyes narrow and she puts her glasses down on the counter in a clear 'ready for a fight' stance, which somehow turns me on even more. What the fuck is going on with me?

"Well dear customer, I will answer the second half of your question—you know, because of your bizarre foray into my wardrobe choices, having only met me about two minutes ago. For your information, Avril is actually two years older than me. She is also a badass bitch who can wear whatever the hell she wants. As for the first half of your question, pompous asses like yourself are probably used to the royal 'we'. I am still awaiting your Karen-like-requests, but the day is young."

That does it—it doesn't matter how hot she is—and my chord snaps. I am not interested in spending another minute being insulted by a wannabe skater girl.

"Is this how you talk to paying customers? I am surprised this shop is still in business! I am this close to walking out the door, but I have to say—I'm even closer to opening a bottle of scotch while talking to you!"

At this, she starts laughing. A loud crystalline laugh, which somehow makes her more beautiful. But crazy is crazy. Do NOT put your dick in crazy!

"Jeez," she says struggling to breathe, "that was one of the most 'Karen' things you could have said! Will you also be wanting to talk to the manager? Maybe leave a scathing Yelp review? Please make my day!" She bats her long eyelashes at me mockingly.

At her amusement, my anger just goes up a notch but I won't give her the satisfaction of continuing the game—despite it being quite entertaining. My cock sure seems to think so and just imagines those nice lips on it. Maybe while I make a fist out of her ponytail and see tears in those bright eyes as I explode down her throat.

Or perhaps I could just fuck her on this counter. It appears to be the right height, I assess after a quick glance, which makes her raise an eyebrow at me in confusion.

"Oh, it is very tempting, skater girl"—damn, now she has a nickname—"but how about you get that ass off that chair and find me a shirt?"

DJ

That conceded asshole! Hot asshole, but what a dick! Issuing me orders like I am his subject, and he is my master.

Though by the snug fit of the custom Armani gray suit on his six-foot three frame, he could be 'mastering' me around in a different context if it weren't for the obvious 'he is a douche' vibe.

Damn those green eyes sparkling at me. Damn that light brown hair—the kind that turns blond in the sun—falling in messy waves around his tanned face and his short, dark beard. The man looks like an extremely hot older rocker in an expensive three-piece suit, with a watch that costs more than a house—and is randomly running an hour behind. And all I would like, if he weren't a giant ass, is to help him change his shirt. Maybe while licking his chest and abs. I suspect there is at least a six-pack hidden under that coffee-stained shirt. But enough objectifying, he needs a little lesson in humility. After the year I've had, I have plenty of energy for a little sparring session.

"Ah dear customer," I seethe in a sweet voice as I get out of my chair and round the counter towards him. "There is nothing in the world I could possibly do besides assisting you, as you've asked so nicely."

I adjust my shirt with a frown. I need to get back at my nephew for making me wear this ridiculous outfit, ill-timed to the one day when I had to help out my brother, Marcus, in the store.

The customer moves back a few steps and I stop about a foot from him, giving him my best 'just die' glare. He appears taller now, and wide. Like a Greek god staring down at me as I barely reach his shoulder.

Get it together DJ!

"Why Avril, you are shorter in real life—maybe you need a stepladder to get to the top shelf!" He grins at me. "This whole angry-chick vibe is 'delightful'," he says while doing air quotes, "but I really need to get out of your charming little shop."

"Not my shop!" I snap. "However, feel free to help your-self to anything on the top shelf. All old guys pick from there for their retirement parties or bingo."

He moves a half step toward me with a scowl. The faint crinkles around his eyes and forehead make him even hot-ter, if possible. He smells intoxicating too, musky cologne and something else... Maybe fuel? It doesn't matter, it is all HIM and I am having trouble concentrating but continuc my death stare thanking the stars he can't tell my panties are wet.

I cross my arms and hold my ground, lifting my chin at him in challenge.

"Avril, I am 38 not 80! How about you go back behind your counter? I will pick my own damn shirt as I see that customer service was not part of your training."

"No way douchebag, nobody puts Baby back in the corner. You wanted me off my chair. Well, here I am." I make a step toward him, and we are now almost touching, both of us staring angrily at each other. I say nothing else. Just shoot him a 'fuck you' smile.

"Douchebag? What are you sixteen? Maybe you can come with some better insults for what is..." he looks around Marcus's shop, "your only client. Those Yelp reviews will not write themselves, you know; I am not sure if I have enough ammo besides your not-so-charming personality and lame jokes."

Lame jokes? The jackass! My zingers are amazing.

"Hmm, better insults you say? Oh boy..." I start, but he cuts me off, his eyes sparkling. His smell is intoxicating. That whiff of fuel hidden behind his expensive cologne makes me want to climb him like a tree. Those biceps I can see even closer now and his giant hands he has on his hips do not help either.

"Man."

"Excuse me?"

"I am a man, not a boy," he says in a deep growly voice. My panties just melted, as that was probably the sexiest thing I ever heard.

"Uh OK caveman, maybe I'll find you some wood to chop out back to make a fire as we are all out of clubs." I manage to add. At least my brain has a few operational cells to avoid making a fool of myself and throw myself at the tantalizing jerk standing way too close to me and glowering at me with the heat of a thousand suns.

That pulls a full smile from him and darn if my last brain cells didn't just stampede to my vagina as she decided that those white teeth and the dimple in his left cheek were cause for celebration.

"Avril, where are these insults? I'm expecting at least three, since I won't be expecting a shirt anytime soon. Maybe never at this rate."

His wit makes it even worse, and I need a strategic retreat, definitely a cold shower. Turning towards the most expensive shirt section, I start to go through the hangers.

"Let's see caveman,"—and now we both have nicknames—"as 'douchebag' is too pedestrian for you, you do know you bring everyone so much joy... you know, when you leave the room."

He huffs, more amused than anything, and follows me towards the merchandise. Glancing again at his suit, I pick a light pink shirt Marcus sewed when he was feeling happy.

"Here, I am sure you can pull off pink. Your face is just fine, but we'll have to put a bag over that personality."

At that, he starts full on laughing. This couldn't have gone worse. He has a full, deep laugh, which messes with me and makes me want to keep on launching insults at him, so he never stops.

Get it together DJ. No more assholes for you, the last few years were enough! I need to focus on getting my career back on track and getting back at my ex-husband for the shit he put me through. I shouldn't be allowing Chris-fucking-Hemsworth to make me all hot and bothered.

"Skater girl, I can... *pull*.... anything I want." That sounded like, again, he meant a different sort of 'pulling'. "Lovely. We finally got to an actual shirt. I need to be at Giorgio's for 1pm and it's across town," he comments, changing direction abruptly and getting the garment from me. He then takes his jacket and vest off and starts unbuttoning his shirt and holy hell, I almost pass out—muscles everywhere—but manage to croak.

"Fitting room over there. No need for the strip show we take Visa."

His naughty smile is back on, maybe with a tint of mischief this time, like he just figured out what button to push. All I can do is stand still as he passes by me way too close and he whispers in my ear, "I am sure you can *take* everything I got, but right now I really need to get changed and out of here."

Frozen on the spot, goose bumps break out all over my skin as he gets in the booth, and I pull the curtain securely behind him.

"You worried you'll see me naked, Avril?" The man chuckles from the fitting room. "If you want to help me change, you are more than welcome."

"No," I answer brusquely, "I imagine you are more than capable." I bite my lower lip, realizing what an opening I just gave him. "Simply putting a barrier between myself and your cheesy lines."

"Hmm, cheesy lines you say?" That deep rumble in his tone makes my thighs clench together. "*Capable* I am, indeed. Just say the word and I'll *thoroughly* demonstrate. You know," he continues in the same trend, "I was feeling a little *off* today, but you *turned* me right *on*."

I puff at the stupid line he knew damn well was cheesy, but he used it anyway, making me smile. I force my lips back down, not wanting to show how he got to me.

Suddenly, a random thought crosses my almost blank mind... the son of a bitch is trying to unbalance me with his flirting. I was letting him get to me! Damn him for looking like Thor's more handsome brother with his long legs, strong arms, and annoying emerald eyes.

And being funny is absolutely unacceptable.

"Hey douche canoe—that's three insults, by the way," I comment casually. I stand next to the full-length drape luckily stopping my lady bits from having a viewing party, or who knows what I would do. "I really hope you weren't checking *your* watch when you said 1pm. From what I can see, even a Patek Philippe watch can be an hour slow, and Giorgio's doesn't hold a reservation more than 15 minutes."

The clothes ruffling behind the screen stops abruptly. A couple minutes of absolute silence grates my nerves before I hear a loud "Fuck it" which puts another smile on my face. But then I am speechless and frozen on the spot as he pulls the curtain open, and I get a full frontal view of his bare chest and the sexiest sleeve tattoos I've ever seen. All my control goes out the window.

JON

My first thoughts were 'how does a shop assistant know what watch I have and what a two-star Michelin restaurant's waiting period is'. But they were quickly overridden by the fact that I completely missed my lunch meeting. Hopefully Mike was covering. Even worse, I have been hard ever since 'Avril' turned towards me and started throwing verbal daggers at me.

This woman might as well have turned on a switch in my dick as it can't seem to get enough of her, and I don't blame it. Those tits she unintentionally pushed up when she crossed her arms, and that round bottom she showed me as she turned to find my shirt in those ridiculous shorts for a woman clearly around 35, almost made me come in my pants. I was lucky the shirts were not on a lower shelf, as I couldn't have kept myself in check if she bent over.

Then there's the back talk and zingy one-liners. If she weren't unexpectedly funny and obviously smart, I would have left the store after the first salvo. Instead, I chose to have a little fun with her.

Her cheeks were getting redder the more she was hurling repartees at me. All I could think was if her ass would get as red if I were to spank her. I wanted to spank her for all the sass coming out of her mouth. And that mouth! I only wanted to mess with her a bit by flirting, but now all I can think of is those pouty lips and angry eyes. The coconut smell of her shampoo almost brought me down.

"Fuck it!" I exclaim and throw the curtain open, halfway through changing, with my old shirt on the floor. I need to do something about this insane attraction to the shop assistant. I have a reckless impulse to see if she has the same conundrum as I. To see if there is something more between us.

She is staring at me, mouth agape, but soon her eyes slowly rove down from my chest to my abs before finally noticing the outline of my hard cock in my pants. Then, as I practically hold my breath, in the reverse motion, she gets another glance, then her eyes are back on mine. Everything stills for what seems like forever as neither of us make a move.

"Fuck it!" she says, then lunges at me.

Her mouth is on mine, and my lips open to let her tongue in. My hands are on her ass, lifting her as she wraps her legs around my waist. Her taste is intoxicating, as I kiss her back hard. She responds with little mewls which spur me on.

I turn us, put her against the wall and use one of my hands to grab her ponytail. My tongue is going crazy around hers; our kiss is all-consuming. We are fighting for the upper hand but neither of us really want to win. My erection presses against her core and I roll my hips so she can feel everything she is doing to me. She moans, her nails scraping against my bare back as she sucks on my tongue, making me go insane.

My cock is straining my pants like never before and if I don't get inside her in the next 30 seconds, I will blow my load. She flexes her center over my dick, knowing damn well what she's doing. Our kisses turn frantic, just licking and teeth and tongues, burning heat between us exploding with every movement.

"Shorts... off!" I gasp, lowering her but continuing kissing her. I have one hand still holding her ponytail and the other struggling to find the button on her shorts.

"Cock... out!" She counters, breaking off our hot-as-fuck kiss as she unclasps her own button and pulls her shorts and sexy little lace panties down, turning to the wall and pushing her juicy bottom towards me.

"Fuckin' hell that sass!" I gasp and spank that ass, receiving a heated glare from her as I get my wallet from my back pocket, get a condom, break the wrapper with my teeth and roll it on. I stare at her perfect bottom for one second before grabbing her ponytail again. Aligning my cock to her entrance, I feel the wetness around her folds and slam into her to the hilt in one go. I am triumphant as it is her turn to gasp, but also awed by her tight cunt that's grasping me like a vise.

"Fuck, you are so wet!" I cry out, thrusting into that crushing pussy. I get even harder when I see the red palm-shape I left on her cheek.

"What can I say?" she asks, pushing back as I plunge, making it a thousand times hotter, "cavemen with no manners turn me on."

"Yeah, Avril. I'll show you caveman!" My strokes get harder and harder. I hold her hips, hoping I'll leave finger marks on her so everyone knows she's mine.

My brain has a fritz... mine? I just met this woman, and I still don't know her name!

I am pulled back to the moment as she moves her right hand from the wall. She puts two of her fingers in her mouth, licks them, before pressing them to her clit, rubbing herself.

"Shit, that is so hot," I pant.

"Yeah? How about this?" She moves her hand lower, touching my balls as my cock is still sinking into her magic slit.

"Fuck, fuck, fuck that was.... I can't stop!" I chant four-letter words as I move my hand on her clit and we massage her nub together. I pump her in a frenzy, getting closer to coming with every movement.

"Fuck, I am so close, do not stop!" She pants, and I feel her getting tighter and tighter around my dick.

I pull on her ponytail as she arches her back, bringing her close to my front, and as I feel her throbbing and starting to come, I bite on her shoulder. She screams loudly, her pussy strangling my cock. That scream makes me lose it as well and I come and come so hard I see stars, cum filling the condom. All I can think is how I wish I could fill her instead. A flash of anticipation of having my release leak down her thighs rattles me.

We are both heaving like we ran a half marathon. My head rests on her shoulder, her with her t-shirt still on and me with my trousers around my ankles when we hear a man's voice.

"DJ are you still here? I'll be right down, and you can go!"

"Shit! My brother's back!" She gulps, pulling herself away and getting her shorts back on. I wrap the condom in a tissue and throw it in the bin as she gets her sex-hair in order and turns to smirk at me again. "That was fun caveman, don't forget your shirt."

Before I can add anything, she leaves the fitting room, pulling the curtain behind her. She leaves me literally holding my dick as I stare at where she just was. Little minx just got fucked and left!

I'm unsure if I am mad or impressed!

By the time I get myself dressed—that pink shirt is seriously well-tailored, and Avril picked exactly my size—and exit the cabin, she is nowhere in sight.

Damn, it's not Avril; it's DJ. Funny again how she has a name fit for a teenager when that woman got my blood pumping unlike anybody else.

A dark-haired young man in an impeccable black shirt and vest, is now behind the counter. He is a bit shorter than me and leaner. He resembles a swimmer, nothing like his bombshell sister with curves in all the right places but... I should probably stop thinking about her curves when her brother narrows his eyes at me in a move that reminds me of her.

"Hello... sir..." he welcomes me tentatively, "didn't realize there was a customer in the store. I see DJ has been helpful. That pink works very well with your charcoal Armani."

"Indeed," I say, "she was extremely... helpful... eventually," I comment diplomatically, though I remind myself how customer service was not her strong suit. That mouth definitely is.

"Umm, if you say so." He appears to know exactly what type of PR nightmare his sister is. "Let me ring that up for you."

"It's great tailoring." I change the subject since I think discussing how his sibling was of assistance is not something I want to bring up. "Do you have other styles? I would also like to look at some suits someday. The one in the window is great."

He stares again at my Armani, hopefully trying to gauge what my style is, and not pondering if I was impaling his sister on my dick ten minutes ago.

"Sure thing, we have lots of options for you! Do you want to set an appointment, or I can come to your... office," he says cautiously, looking at my outfit again "with a sample selection? Here is my business card if your assistant wants to make an appointment for you."

Clever guy. With one look at me he pinned me as working in a busy office and as someone who rarely makes his own appointments. Though thinking about Anya's skills or lack thereof makes me groan. I need to fire her when

I get back, as missing my appointment isn't acceptable, despite the outcome of the day. Speaking of...

"Is... DJ... still around? I would like to thank her for assisting." Hopefully I sound bored, but the guy is no fool as he gives me a pointed look.

"I am going to stop you right here. I know exactly how 'helpful' my sister is and if I didn't have a blasting toothache, she would have never been here. Normally Monday is our slowest day. I didn't think we would get any customers. So, knowing she isn't exactly 'customer friendly' and by your fake uninterested tone, I will assume that it's not a 'discussion' you want to have with her. However, she isn't having the best year, so I would appreciate it if you moved on. If you still want to talk about suits, give me a ring, but if not, it is what it is."

Goddamn. Forceful comebacks must run in the family. I appreciate the brother's spunk. He's willing to lose an obviously rich customer for his sister.

"No worries, man. I won't interfere, thanks for the warning. Once I get a new assistant, I will have them give you a ring," I respond. Putting his card in my wallet, I pay for my shirt and leave the shop.

As I exit the store, I look at the card, hoping to get DJ's last name, but all I get is 'Marcus's Tailoring' and a phone number on the back of it. And I do not know why that upset me. I just spent half an hour with her; I was not looking for more. Hell, I wasn't even expecting a quickie in a fitting room, especially with her attitude.

I do not need the complication, and that hellion is nothing if not that. Sex was fantastic, but pursuing a mouthy shop girl—woman— even one who is bold and clever, is definitely not what I need right now. So even if something in me makes me want to check out who Marcus is and find out more about his sister, I force myself to go back to the office.

DJ

As my mother sets the table on Sunday, I take a moment to look around her house. It's a lovely cottage I bought her last year, with large windows overlooking a magnificent garden and pool, and a veranda where our family gathers for lunch from time to time. My nephew's laughter is sounding off the walls as he plays on his Xbox and my mother's nagging is coming from the kitchen.

"*Mi hija* you need to add more salt, it has no taste otherwise." She chastises my older sister, who somehow at 37 still needs indications—in my mom's opinion—to make a recipe she has been making with her since she was 13. My *mamá* at least gave up trying to teach me after a couple of kitchen incidents, but Laura still gets a stern teacher every Sunday we get together.

Marcus is playing backgammon with Uncle Antonio at the table, and I am nursing my mojito in *mamá*'s rocking chair, absolutely NOT thinking about green eyes and sleeve tattoos hidden behind an Armani suit.

I still can't believe I jumped one of Marcus's customers, nor that we banged in the fitting room. Since Richard, I went on a few dates, but none of them seemed to challenge me as that messy-haired jackass on Monday. That massive cock pumping me as he claimed my hips and smacked my ass... let's just say my vibrator had quite a week as I recalled Monday's lunchtime events.

When he opened that curtain, all I saw was miles of skin, tribal tattoos on his arms, that six-pack I was expecting and a most delicious happy trail... and then I could see how hard he was as he was looking at me... Well, I snapped and poured years of frustration into eating him alive.

"DJ, you seem a bit distant," Marcus mentions, "are you OK?"

I nod, breathing through my nose and massaging my temples.

"Nothing Marcus, just big day tomorrow, need to get all the money off those guys at McAv after the whole Richard debacle." I lie and touch the bite mark he left through my t-shirt on my shoulder which has almost faded now, but has been reminding me of my moment of insanity all week.

"Hmm." Marcus's eyebrow goes up, not believing a word out of my mouth. "So has nothing to do with Thor in the shop the other day?"

"What Thor?" Uncle Antonio perks up from the anchor play he likes. "Does our little DJ have an admirer?" he continues like I'm 10, not 35!

But just as a 10-year-old, I roll my eyes at him. "No admirer, *Tío* Antonio. I helped Marcus in the store on Monday and one of the customers bought a shirt."

My younger sibling moves closer to me and whispers, so my uncle doesn't hear, "I think there was a bit more going on based on your red face and quick escape from the store when I got back from the dentist. However, he looked like he could lift you with one arm and drag you to his expensive man-cave, maybe a sex dungeon? Do you want his name? He paid by card. OK, that may be a bit stalker-ish and probably breaks a few privacy laws, but I won't tell if you don't," he winks.

"Yeah Marcus, maybe we don't invade the man's privacy for fuck's sake!" I shake my head at him. "But ignoring the legal implications you of all people should know of, I really don't want to get involved right now. Frankly, he was an arrogant ass. No need to pursue that *pendejo*." I keep telling myself as I get out of the rocking chair.

"I need mentally prepare for tomorrow's meeting, which I need to ace to get back some of the money Richard got off me. Let us leave jerk-Thor in Asgard for today. Maybe after tomorrow, I will reconsider." I head away from the porch, towards the pool, needing a bit of space from my family.

Sitting on the bench at the other end of *mamá*'s garden, I admire the quiet and greenery around me. Again, I wonder what possessed me to assault a guy in the shop.

Hearing movement beside me, I recognize the click-clack of her cane against the footpath, and my big sis Laura slides next to me on the bench and puts her arm around me. Her dark hair with red ends brushes my shoulder and the smell of her reminds me of growing up and being held when I cried or just because I needed it.

"So lil D, man trouble? I saw you and Marcus whispering, and you were a tad... blushing."

"I thought you were supposed to be taught how to make *ropa vieja* for the millionth time. Or was it how to cut an onion?" I tease her.

"Ha ha—it's not like you know how to do either DJ," the bitch counters. "Seriously now, you seem a bit lost. Do you want to talk about it with the sibling with a vagina?"

That makes me smile—she is two years older than me and has a kid, but somehow has the dirtiest mouth on her, but I always loved having my big sister to talk sex and boyfriends with. This is a big part of me wanting to come back to Florida after my divorce. Sundays like this, when Marcus makes fun of me, *mamá* cooks and mumbles and Laura wants to take care of us. She—damned wise older sister—has a point, though; I need to talk about it with someone, and at least here, far from the kitchen, my mom can't listen in.

"Oh vagina-sister, I may or may not have mm... how to say this... have had a one-lunch-stand in Marcus's shop." I put my head in my hands in mock despair as my kin starts giggling loudly.

"So? Besides the obvious 'eww I will not be sitting on his counter ever again', it's not really uncommon for you to find yourself a man to pass the time with. Especially now, you need to find distractions wherever you can. But again... please tell me you cleaned the counter?"

"Relax—the counter is pretty safe—though my 'lunch' was staring at it a bit weirdly, come to think about it. The fitting room wall, however, may have an imprint of my ass," I continue sheepishly as Laura grins at me.

"Hi5 sis!"—with actual high five. "That sounds awesome! I still do not understand why you're out here moping. Unless... shit—you liked him?" she gasps, her eyes wide open.

I take a big swig of my mojito and look out into the distance.

"I did not! We literally had a ten-minute conversation, then I jumped his bones. By 'conversation', I mean bickering with the entitled jerk who couldn't wait for one entire minute until I emailed my accountant before being all demanding that I find him a shirt! Perhaps he was a bit funny. OK, he was very funny and, in my opinion, he thought I was pretty funny as well. And hot—Lau, he was so hot..."

"I see... so a customer demanded service, and you... serviced him?" I roll my eyes at her, and she pinches my side. "So, are you going to go find him or what? He seems to have given you some visual and verbal gratification on top of a good dickin'. By the way—who was on top?" She snickers at me but then changes her tune. "You know I appreciate a good hump-and-dump as much as any other girl, but what's the harm in seeing if there is something more there? I know you, and you wouldn't be thinking about him if it was just a cock-du-jour."

"I don't know Laura... I am not sure if it was insta-lust or what. And with all the stuff going on, I think I'd be mad to go trying to find a guy now."

"OK, how about this—you go have your meeting tomorrow, fleece them for all its worth, then let's get very, very, very drunk! Then maybe you can delve illegally into Marcus's accounts and find your man's details and call him for some more bickering!" She gets up and pulls me with her, dragging me back to the house just as her son Javi starts yelling for her.

"Jeez, I think I am on board with the drinking. You look like you need it too. But I think I'll leave the hacking for another day. I am so glad both my siblings believe we should just break a few laws so easily."

"Well, lil D, anything for you. You know that right? You want us to find you a tall handsome shopper, we will bring him to you... naked and oiled up, of course."

Before I throttle her, my mom catches us both being idle, so we get corralled into lunch prep again, but an image of an oiled, tanned, annoying man sneaks into my mind and puts down roots. Next to the image of that darn dimple when he laughs at my insults.

JON

Dark silky locks, brown eyes staring at me as I feed my throbbing shaft to those soft lips and she gags on me, but I keep pumping her mouth, harder and harder. I imagine grabbing her hair as I hold her, using her as she fingers herself while taking all my length.

I fist my dick more and more in the shower, envisioning that impertinent brunette as I have been doing all week, as forgetting her seems impossible. My hand moves faster and faster and I come all over my tiles as I visualize erupting down her throat, cum leaking out of a corner of her mouth when I am spent.

"Fuck!" I yell with my release.

As I dress slowly as I button up my white shirt to go with my black two-piece Brioni suit, I think of her again. Not just that ass I didn't get a chance to fuck, but her brazenness and intensity, which call to me like a siren song. I imagine how I will take her next, either hard and fast or painfully slow, until she begs for me. That thought appeals to me most, seeing her moaning my name, wanting me to fill her up but me not giving in to her ask, just having her wanton and needy for my cock.

Though mostly I think more about asking her what is her real job? What does she do for fun besides grilling customers?

I realize that after work today I will call that tailor myself for a new suit, and definitely for his last name. At this point, I would actually uncomplicate my life if I were to find her, as at least I would stop obsessing and get some work done. Perhaps seeing her again would stop my brain from going into overdrive when I see how obnoxious she is in the real world. Maybe she is boring, and only talks about knitting. Or maybe she doesn't return her shopping cart or a million other things which would drive me insane.

My morning routine is simple. I already ran 5k before the shower, and a quick breakfast and coffee set me for the day, as I sit at my kitchen island, enjoying the soft light through the folding glass doors. My house is not huge, just a couple of bedrooms and a study upstairs and a semi-open plan downstairs, and my favorite place, the deck off the kitchen where I usually spend my evenings reading. I don't need a lot of space, and I abhor the thought of living in a soulless condo. Or worse, a Florida-style white modern house with more glass than necessary. Nothing inside my home screams CEO. I enjoy the warm feel of my cream couches or my white and gray kitchen. Or the navy tones in my bedroom, which are more about comfort and a good night's sleep than fancy designs.

My driver awaits in front of the townhouse in my Range Rover for my ride to work. Which saves me time as I check my emails and field answers on the loss of the tire supplier last week the press just got word of. The hell with Miranda Lexington from LexAviation, undercutting me with my oldest supplier. We need tires to get our planes delivered. Every day our stocks are getting lower, so the deal with a new distributor is critical. I clench my phone, thinking this programmer better be as good as Mike says, as I definitely need a win to push in that bitch's face.

Anya is nowhere near her desk as I arrive at work, so I see myself to coffee and sit in front of my computer screens, dialing into a call with some of our Asian suppliers. Time flies as I counter their offers and poke holes at their manicured progress reports as they try to hide their errors behind pretty fonts and pictures. Luckily, I have been in the aerospace industry for a while and can read through their bullshit. Damn right you will 'take it away' and fix it.

"Umm sir," Anya calls from outside my office, "Mrs. Jones wants to let you know that as you weren't in at 9, she is waiting in her office with Ms. Jara."

"What? Wasn't that tomorrow?" I realize it's almost ten and if the interview was scheduled for 9, I will look like a massive jerk. "Why didn't you greet her? Or better yet, tell me before now?"

"Umm sir, I didn't appreciate she was your interview sir, it just said 'meeting Jara' in the calendar, and I assumed you would be in conference room 2. I was getting copies of the end-of-quarter report for the Finance team meeting at 1."

31

"Conference room 2? I doubt that very much. That Finance session is hours away, you should staff your desk," I mumble as I check my calendar. It was indeed on the agenda for Monday not Tuesday—don't know why I thought it was tomorrow—and it didn't actually specify a place. That's it, Anya is out the door. Again, I got no phone notifications for the interview either.

I jog down the corridor towards Mike's office, but I slow down as a pair of red-soled black stilettos are visible through her office door. They continue with some sculpted calves and—from what I can see under the frosted pane—a burned-orange dress hem.

I knock briefly and I notice my VP getting up from her chair and opening the door for me. Her guest's long dark brown hair, slightly curled around her shoulders is flowing down her back. A bold colored dress looking amazing against her caramel skin tone and a black blazer catches my eye. However, she isn't turning towards me at all, like I don't even matter. I frown.

"Jon, so glad you managed to handle that emergency in the hangar." Michaela winks exaggeratedly as clearly, she had to invent something, so Ms. Jara didn't realize we completely blew the meeting with her. "Let me introduce you to Dahlia, the most talented programmer in aerospace," she continues sweetly, sucking up to our guest.

Dahlia Jara picks up her Prada bag off the floor and slowly rises from the seat, and as she turns to me, all I can see again is... brown eyes full of fire. The surprise in her gaze matches my own as the hot shop assistant from last week somehow transforms into the hottest woman in the world in a figure-hugging dress, red lips, and wavy hair. The daggers in her eyes return abruptly, however.

"Hangar emergency, was it?" she asks in a similar tone to Mike's, but clearly spotting a cover-up from a mile away.

Michaela slowly looks from her to me and back and continues the intros.

"Jonathan McMaster, our CEO here at McAv Aviation." As I just continue to glower at Avril—uh, DJ—Dahlia and she at me, my VP gently tries for a fake cough, and I wake up and offer her my hand in greeting.

Little minx looks at my palm like it's something off the bottom of her shoe but shakes it, her long delicate fingers with fuck-me red nails I vividly remember scratching my back encompassed in my large hand.

We hold the handshake as the heat we had last week uncoils between us. An electric field is palpable and flares just as the last time at the shop, despite the death glares.

How did I think she would ever be boring?

Mike makes a funny throat noise again, interrupting our stare-a-thon.

"Ms. Jara was just telling me about the latest software she is working on—what was it? Weather predictor?"

"Yes," Dahlia says slowly, breaking away and looking at Mike, "an improved weather predictor reading and processing data from thousands of satellites. It uses statistic interpolation to predict up to 3 days in advance exact conditions in a certain area."

The software sounds fantastic, but something about her makes me just want to poke the bear and I ask.

"We are already using the best-in-industry weather predictor. What makes your software worth our time? The customers of our private jets expect the best. How would yours surpass that?" I know, dick comment, but expecting that flash of fury in her makes my blood heat up. I can feel my VP's face pale as she is shocked by my rudeness.

Dahlia opens her mouth to answer immediately and probably blast me all over the office, but I can see she first takes a breath in a practiced stance. Suspect I was milliseconds away from getting eviscerated, and now just the tint in her cheekbones showing her ire.

"Though 'Cloud9' is an adequate software,", she winces as 'adequate' is clearly not adequate at all in her view, "my code's data accuracy would ensure circa 10% fuel reduction and better cancelation preview."

I hear Michaela gasp in the background as she is checking a ping on her phone but overhears Dahlia's statement, which could save us millions if accurate.

"In that case I suppose you wouldn't have an issue if my team checked your predictions and statistics," I volley with contempt. Ms. Jara assumes quite a lot if she thinks I will just take her at her word when 'Cloud9' is used throughout the aviation industry by all airlines as the benchmark weather software.

She licks those sultry lips and tilts her head, probably preparing to bite mine off.

"If your team are experts in probability calculations, they can obviously have a look. My software, however, is my own. I expect full control and ownership of all programming."

Ownership of the code? Full control? That does it, again this woman is getting my blood pressure through the roof.

"Listen here, Ms. Jara, anything you code on as part of this job is work product so belongs to my company," I growl as I make an aggressive step towards her.

"Listen here, Mr. McMaster," she imitates my tone and holds her position out of sheer arrogance, "your company requested this meeting. I could go to any other of your competitors. Look at Hove's code if you want and tell me who else can replicate that for you, but I won't hold my breath. My code is my own. You can rent exclusive usage, but trust me, it won't be cheap. I really like my Louboutin's," she throws at the end, making my eyes go to her shoes, taking her in as I go.

Fantastic boobs I spot under that blazer, grab-able waist and long legs in those stilettos make me want to toss her on Mike's desk. Better yet, drag her into my office and eat her up.

Or maybe just continue this little fight, as it is her feistiness that captures my attention just as much as her body, maybe even more so.

She gives me a brazen once over as well, but before she can throw some more vitriol at me, my friend interrupts.

"Loving this deathmatch you both got going on here but would appreciate it if you could please stop before you start throwing furniture at each other," my VP says, clearly needing to arbitrate between us.

We shamefully move back from each other, looking at nothing in particular, but Mike continues, "Just got a news alert you really need to see, Jon. Sorry Dahlia, but this affects you too."

DJ

What were the chances of me running into Him again, and what were the chances of him being the CEO of the company I was in discussions with? Pretty high, it seems. He still pushed all my buttons, and I had to resort to every angry management technique I know to not remove the head off his massively wide shoulders. That jackass assumed I would just work for him like a good little worker bee. I am a goddamn rock star, not here to be told what to do by his Holy Hotness.

Arriving at their downtown office this morning—after double and triple checking I had the right day and address—I was impressed by the glass building at the edge of the business district, close enough to the local airport and the McAv factory and testing facilities. Sleek and modern, mostly open plan, done up in bright greens and orange colors with fancy chairs and various areas of comfortable sofas and tables for collaboration sprinkled between desks.

Conference rooms line one side of the floor, and offices with glass doors on the other, probably for management.

When I made it to the CEO's executive assistant desk, the scared young woman, whom I thought was a bit familiar, mumbled some excuse for her boss, who apparently was not ready for me. Ms. Jones showed up out of nowhere and the girl scrammed. I barely caught a look at the EA, but I did notice the freckles on her nose, partially hidden behind some massive, unflattering glasses, and blonde hair, which could use a wash, in a low bun.

The VP, however, was a lovely lady in a well-suited gray dress and pumps, who was genuinely excited to see me but somehow also happy to cover for Dick McDickface. I assume he obviously forgot about our session this morning, probably being caught in some penis measuring contest.

Unfortunately, just as last week at the shop, the Man was still hotter than sin. A black suit and a white shirt with no tie, with an inkling of his golden chest showing as the top button was undone. Again, with his saucy green eyes and long-ish hair I wanted to grab him with both hands and drag his mouth to lick his lips as he pummels my pussy.

Also, as last week, he is a complete jerk! After his last comment I was just about to say the job would not work out and walk out of there with my head held high instead of tackling him on the office floor and riding him into oblivion.

But what Michaela said gave me pause.

"Me? What do you mean?" I ask as she picks up the remote and turns on the TV on the wall on a local news station.

The reporter is cheerfully explaining an impromptu press conference from Lex Aviation, a rival airline to McAv, which recently moved its headquarters to Florida from New York. Seeing Jon's anger level rise as he clenches his fists and breathes heavily, I suspect he was not happy at all with the move.

I did actually have a meeting with her two weeks ago, but the CEO there wouldn't budge on owning the software and also something about her gave me the literal creeps. So, I thanked her for her time and walked out. She was quite unhappy with my reluctance to just roll over and hand her my work on a silver platter, without even being recognized for it.

"Ladies and gentlemen, the CEO of Lex Aviation, Miranda Lexington, and her new IT & Data management Director, Richard Simmons."

"What the hell!" Both Jon and I say at the same time and glance at each other, surprised at our common outburst.

"Good morning, so glad you could be here with just half an hour's notice. I know it is unusual, but we just couldn't wait to give you all the good news which will take the aviation world by storm!" Ms. Lexington, with her perfect dark skin and contrasting white pantsuit, is the epitome of perfection, but something in her sleazy smile caused me to be wary of whatever else she was about to say.

"Fucking bitch! What the hell is she pulling?" Jon rumbles next to me.

Back in the conference room, the dark-haired, tall man is sitting by Miranda's side with a brilliant grin. Or as I've been known to call him, a toad of a man, he approaches the microphone and starts, with his perfect baritone voice.

"As some of you are not familiar with me, I am the newly appointed IT and Data management Director here at the best aviation company in the world." Jon huffs at that. "But what you may or may not be aware of is that in the past few years I have been working on a new and exciting software you all should hear about!"

I blanch holding on to the chair in front of me. "Oh no," I gasp and Mike and Jon stare at me... "the slimy snake!" I put it into words with uncontainable anger.

"The software, I like to call 'Zephyr'"—jackass he stole the name as well—"will be the best weather predictor in the industry and will minimize fuel consumption by 20%!"

"What the actual fuck, the son of a bitch! My goddamn ex-husband!" My wrath was now beyond limits as I approach the TV, but I couldn't hear what he was talking about anymore, just seeing his snarky smirk and Miranda's fake-ness on display.

"Care to explain why your ex is announcing a better weather predictor than you just tried to peddle, but for my biggest competitor?" Jon is prancing around the office absolutely furious, but his assumptions were about to land him on his ass.

"Cool your jets, boss-hole," I say through my teeth. "He does not have the software and no way it can save 20%. What he has is the court-mandated half the code I wrote."

"What? You came to sell me half a code when your ex has the other half? And you had the gall to ask for ownership?" His green eyes were burning with displeasure.

"Oh, get down from your high horse! He managed to convince his judge buddy in L.A. to get half in the divorce as presumably he 'helped' create it. But the idiot didn't think to specify which half or how it will be portioned!"

"So?" He is again towering over me with hands against his waist in his favored superman pose which, on a different day, would cause me to melt.

"So... genius..." I wave my hand about and poke him with my finger—damn those hard pecs. "It means he got a randomized half version of my code! It should take him years to put it back together! I can do it in a couple of months, as unlike him, I actually created it! I have no idea what possessed them to announce it now. They are years away from anything viable, and no way is the savings realistic... he is full of shit!"

"How you expect me to believe that today of all days they decided to present it when you showed here for an interview? How do I know this isn't some setup between you and your husband to get access to my system while he gets with that shark, Miranda, and you take both our money?"

"Listen here, you jerk; I would not work with Richard, the smarmy bastard if he had the last computer in the world! He can burn in hell for all it's worth—he is nothing more than a common thief!"

Before we both much into further yelling at each other, however, Ms. Jones intervenes and literally separates us as though we are children on the playground.

"Right kids, I think your tempers stop you both from seeing what I'm seeing! This may be a golden opportunity for all of us here!"

We stare at her and then glare at each other.

She continues, "So Dahlia, shall I assume all you would like after this morning—besides to kick Jon in the nuts..."

"Hey!" he argues, "I am sitting right here!"

But she ignores him. "Is to make sure your ex-husband is ridiculed in front of everyone you know and made to crawl back to whatever hole he got out of?"

"Yes, that sounds about right," I admit, slightly impressed.

"And Jon, I know you, the only thing you have been trying for the past 15 years is to make sure Miranda and her company are burned to the ground and then buried in a lime-coated deep grave?"

"That was oddly specific, Mike, but it wouldn't hurt," he says, and his fury diminishes a bit.

"Well then, kids," she adds, blatantly looking at both of us, "it seems that besides the obvious... affliction... between you two—which I am not about to unravel right now—you are in an 'enemy of my enemy is my friend' situation. Jon needs to overtake Lex Aviation and after this morning's spectacle, the best way of doing it is launching this software earlier than those nincompoops. Dahlia needs some time to repack her software and an aviation company to test and use it and make sure everyone knows that it was her—with her double masters from Berkely—not her college dropout ex-hubby who wrote it." I noticed she specifically mentioned my qualifications, no doubt for Jon's benefit, who probably didn't bother to read my CV.

Jon and I carry on staring at each other, waiting for one of us to break the stalemate we found ourselves in, as Mike's words made perfect sense, but neither wants to admit it out loud. All the fight between us pointed towards our rivals would really be something else.

"Fine!" I relent. "Fifty mil down payment and three years exclusive usage of the software for McAv plus a percentage of savings," and put out my hand.

"You are insane, skater girl! Absolutely crazy! Twenty million down payment and ten years exclusive usage! We also want franchise options to other airlines!" Back in Superman pose he goes trying to intimidate me, but he is in for a surprise when Mike takes his hand and clasps it against mine. Electricity jolts us both again, but we don't react.

"Twenty-five mil down, five years exclusive usage and the percentage and the franchising—we can agree later," she closes the deal for both of us.

Begrudgingly I grunt, "Deal."

"Deal," he mutters angrily. "NOT looking forward to working with you, Ms. Jara!"

"Feeling is mutual, Mr. McMaster! Ms. Jones, thanks for refereeing. Please email me the contract." I throw the last word in, then pick up my bag and leave the office, managing not to slam the door or punch him in the throat. With difficulty.

Jon

The week continued downhill after my hell of a morning between the 12 rounds with Dahlia and the announcement from Miranda. Another supplier—this time carpets—asked to have a meeting next week to review our contract. Again something smelled fishy, so I put a call to my PI to make sure all our security measures are in place and the firewall is still working. My Security team here also reassures me that everyone's phones are checked and cameras are stickered, and nobody can take any pictures without the proper forms. But it seems we continue to have a leak.

By Thursday I was using one wall in my office to bounce my stress ball off it when Mike walks in, her navy business suit and silver short hair in all their glory, but with a scowl on her face I haven't seen in a while.

"Well... if it isn't the CEO of a company who employs over 5000 people," she mocks my voice on the phone from last week, "you literally had one mission, and that was to not mess up the session with Dahlia Jara. Do you want to tell me why I had to send you both to your corners?"

I turned my head to her, remembering—as if I could forget—those blazing eyes and the firebrand of a woman they came with. All week I tried to erase her from my head—again—as what I asked for happened: a reason to stop thinking of her, and her working for me is the best of them all. That was a line I never crossed ever since I took over McAv, and was not about to start now, especially not when Dahlia Jara was still a live grenade with baggage to boot.

"None of your business, Mike. She just rubs me the wrong way and I can't seem to stop myself from aggravating her!"

"Mm..." She nods, unconvinced. "From where I was sitting looked less aggravating and more like foreplay in the form of pulling on the girl's pigtails. Anything I need to warn HR of?"

"Nothing to say—not interested at all! She's my employee now, not going anywhere near her, especially with the mess with her husband and Miranda."

"The gentleman doth protests too much, methinks, but I will let it go for now as she won't be around the office much, anyway."

"What do you mean?" I ask, forgetting to feign indifference, as the thoughts of DJ's behind in that dress... those heels... maybe of her wearing nothing but those heels as I spread her on the conference room table have been haunting my dreams since Monday. More so, my days were spent going through her software proposal, and marveling at how her mind works.

Mike has a less than flattered reaction to my excited question, shaking her head and removing an inexistent lint off her pants.

"Good thing you aren't interested, Jon," she smiles at me. "She sent back an edited version of the contract where she requests to work remotely at least 4 days a week. Don't think that's an issue, seeing as her job is basically behind computer screens."

"She WHAT? No way she's getting 4 days to sit in her pajamas and mooch off my money!"

"Jon, I think you are overreacting. She doesn't need supervision and all her work can be done remotely," my VP is trying to dissuade me gently. "We would also need to find her space in some of the upstairs' offices. The IT department is really unsavory—nobody would like to work down there, especially not someone of her caliber."

But I was too far gone to properly listen to anything Mike said. The audacity of that woman to come into my company and demand special treatment! She should be in the office so I can see what my millions are buying!

I pull my email app on my laptop and start typing in anger, but I feel my VP rolling her eyes at me.

Dear Ms. Jara,

Ms. Jones has highlighted your request to work from home for at least 4 days a week. However, it is against company policy 176/45-2019 to allow this demand. All new starters need to be in the office full time for the first 6 months to ensure adherence to business processes, familiarization to procedures and team integration.

Your supplication is hereby refused. Please be in the office starting tomorrow between the business hours of 9 and 5 pm.

Best regards,

Jon McMaster

CEO McAv Aviation

There, all processes are applied. She had no way of fighting a company procedure. Though at least a part of me wanted to see her try. Maybe see that red coloring in her cheeks. Maybe hear that razor sharp mind come up with some flaying words.

Michaela shakes her head at me, mumbling something along the lines of "Why do I even bother," but I realize I still have a useless EA I need to discuss with her.

"So, when are you finding me a new assistant? Can't be that hard!"

"HR is on the case Jon, not really my job as I keep trying to remind you... they are culling through the applicants and should have a shortlist for you by the end of next week. I think you will survive with Anya for a few more weeks."

"Come on Mike, you know you are my right-hand woman, couldn't do the job without you taking care of it all! You'd think I can endure my assistant! Yesterday she erased half the slides I was prepping for the meeting with X-Access. Good thing I thought of showing them the assembly line instead, which actually worked better. Old-boy Franken loved it, otherwise we would have been in trouble!"

"Oh Jon, don't worry, Anya will be out of your hair soon enough. However, I hope whatever you wrote in that email to Dahlia won't come back to bite you in the ass. We need her to finish that code." Grasping my stress ball again, I was beginning to think I shouldn't have written the email, and definitely shouldn't be eagerly awaiting the consequences.

"I know, and I am sure she will. Hey, isn't that Cole?" I flag down the young blond guy wandering around the open-plan desk area outside my private office, looking a bit lost.

"Jon, how's it going? Haven't seen you in months!" he says as he walks in to shake my hand. "Hey mom, I was searching for you. We need to discuss some party prep stuff."

"Sure, I will be right there," my VP confirms.

"It's all good," I answer. "What are your plans now that you finished college? Any job leads?"

I've known her youngest son for a long time. For a while he used to follow me around like a puppy, but I haven't seen much of him in the past few years as he was studying in Colorado. So, I am glad he is finally back, and by the party she is paying for, so is Mike.

"Umm," he hesitates, glancing at his mother. "A few, actually, but still work in progress."

"OK, hope they all pan out. If you need a job, I am sure we can find a new starter role here as well. Ah, and sorry I can't make your celebration. There is this charity thing during the day, and I don't know when it will end." Also, the thought of spending the night with Cole's 20-year-old friends makes me break out in hives.

"That won't be necessary, Jon," Michaela intervenes. "He is looking a bit higher than starter roles. By the way, I must send someone with you to that Julia Li event the following Saturday, as I'll be at my son's party."

"Well, I am sure you'll find someone. I definitely don't want to face those sharks by myself."

"Oh, I have just the person," she smiles conspiratorially. "But for now, I need to see what this urgent issue with the party is."

On that note, they return to her office, leaving me staring at my Outbox, and the hurricane Jara my email will bring.

JON

F riday came around and I had meetings downtown in the morning, but my Friday's afternoons were blocked for my hands-on time in the workshops, where my 1975 Cessna 172 plane was awaiting a rebuild.

I had rented half the minor reworks hangar for my own use. Despite the mountains of Health and Safety documents with every disclaimer known to man which had to be signed, I had my personal airplane in the company's hangar as I did when I was a teenager. I recall fondly those times struggling to fix the even older model and asking the technicians for help as I had no idea what I was doing back then.

I chuckle, reminding myself how they sometimes made fun of me or pulled my leg and sent me for blinker fluid and other inexistent items. It wasn't until I started pranking them right back, switching their tools around or hiding their kit did they embrace me there, not seeing me as the

CEO's son but just a kid needing help. I was almost glad my dad was not interested and left me to my own devices when I was a teenager, as I would have never gotten too close to my staff with him here.

I love working on old planes, selling them after fixing them, nothing like rebuilding an engine to calm me down after another shit week, peppered by memories of long dark brown hair and a burned orange dress, or of ridiculous shorts hugging a stellar bottom. Or of intense comebacks which made me chuckle in the shop and made me feel ridiculously alive on Monday.

Dressed down in overalls and an old t-shirt, grabbing my tool kit, I start on landing gear, leaving the wiring for the flaps to the last minute. I tried doing some work on that before, but I pretty much just made matters worse. I really needed to get an electrician from the factory to come have a look. I didn't have the patience to match all the connectors and re-pin the whole thing.

An hour into stripping the landing gear, my peace is interrupted by a click-clack on the hangar floor, heading towards me at speed.

"What the actual fuck is this email?" an indignant female voice echoes on the walls, causing me to unintentionally smile as I instantly recognize the owner.

"Gooday to you too, Ms. Jara," I say, getting up from under the plane, but as I lift my head, I get a great view of another pair of black high-heeled shoes, this time with little ties around her ankles. Fuck. Me.

"You know you should have steel-toed boots in the hangar, you are a walking code violation," I continue, all the while slowly perusing her tight purple dress and stopping a groan from coming out. She must have been quite furious as she stormed in here and thinking how she got all worked up—and the crimson on her cheekbones—keeps the smile on my face. I wonder, with blood flowing to my groin just imagining it, if my bite mark is visible on her.

Randomly, she has no comeback to that, as she takes me in standing with my overalls tied around my waist, holding an Allen key, and probably with dirt all over my t-shirt.

She may be appalled by the grease monkey in front of her and that causes me to smirk at her as—despite knowing nothing can happen between us again—unbalancing her may become my new hobby.

"You got grease all over your face!" Is what comes out of her mouth, then catches herself as she reminds herself why she's there and continues.

"This policy is full of shit. I'm not a new starter, for fuck's sake! I've been working in aviation for 20 years. I don't need handholding or trust-falls. By the way, you're aware that most of your IT team actually is in Asia, so having me sitting in an empty office only pisses me off. And who the hell uses words like 'hereby' and 'supplication' in an email? Did you crack open a thesaurus or do you think you are in a period drama?"

Those red cheeks are back in force, and I can't stop myself from fixating on the little spitfire's tirade before I too catch myself and remind myself what I was supposed to reply, and that I am her boss. The people in the hangar have stopped working and watch the show with interest. I pick up a clean cloth and wipe my face.

"Policy is policy. So, unless you feel like helping me fix my plane, just trot on back to the office and continue with your keyboard warrior gig," I press on with a dismissing wave at her.

I would have assumed that brush-off would have pissed her off even more and expected a witty riposte—or a slap—but then she grins at me and lifts her chin. It's a clear 'you fucked up and now you are going to pay' signal which makes me wonder if I am about to get hit in the head with my own wrench. Walking slowly around my plane, perusing as if she owns the place, she stops and points at the harnesses hanging out.

"It's clear why you need help here—which five-year-old wired that? My nana could do a better job and she can't see from her left eye."

Some technicians chuckle as my aversion to wiring is well known, but I give them a pointed look.

"It's still under repairs," I dodge and cross my arms.

"For goodness' sake," she mutters and starts looking in her purse for something. Of all the things I was expecting, a connector kit and a multimeter were not anywhere near my list, but she pulls them out from a side pocket, then puts them down next to the bag.

She then goes to the locker and gets a pair of overshoes on top of her pumps while doing a ridiculous chicken dance hopping on each leg. That makes her tits bounce as she clicks the clasp in place high behind her heel. The guys—and some ladies—are suddenly even more interested in the spectacle, but I send some serious 'I am the boss, go back to work' vibes and they pretend to go back to doing what I am paying them for.

"You carry that in your purse?" I erupt, but she stares at me like I am an idiot. Like I am the moron to not even fathom that a millionaire programmer dressed in $1000 shoes and carrying a bag ten times more expensive would cart tools around for kicks.

"Of course I do, duh! Connector kit, multimeter, mini spanner and screwdriver set, pliers," she enumerates. "I have been fixing planes since high school. My second degree is in avionics. I didn't get into software for aviation on a whim, you know." Then, she turns her back to me, gets a hair tie out of her bag, and sets her locks in a haphazard bun, showing her long neck and the top of her shoulders. To shock me even more, as if my cock isn't threatening to burst out of my coveralls just by seeing more of her skin, she climbs the ladder and starts rewiring while humming and completely ignoring me.

I stand there speechless as the image of Dahlia Jara in a purple dress that fits her to the T, golden zipper visible running the full length of her garment, steel cap overshoes over her Jimmy Choo's and holding a flashlight in her mouth while she fits connectors to my airplane is seared in my mind forever. The glasses she slided on her nose don't help either.

The men—myself included—rearrange our dicks in our pants and I personally am thankful I tied the sleeves of my coveralls over my middle, hiding my bulge.

DJ

We work in companionable semi-silence for the next half an hour or so, hot jerk snapping himself out of the trance he fell in while staring at me working on the wires and carrying on his landing gear bearing change. We only talk to swap tools or for me to ask where things are, careful to put everything back in place and not at all sneak a peek at Jon tightening bolts and whatnot, muscles in his arms straining with every twist of the wrench.

When I heard he was in the hangar and I marched in full force, I was fully expecting him to be doing some audits or checking on the crew.

What I was not expecting was a member of Billy Joel's band almost ready to sing 'Uptown girl'—that is if any of the guys in the band would have been a 220lbs bear-man ready to hoist half the Cessna with their bare hands. His enormous, tattooed arms were straining against his white t-shirt, and his narrow waist with his overalls wrapped around it was making me want to unwrap him like a Christmas present. Maybe with my teeth, as he leans against the aircraft.

Get a grip DJ! I tell myself, as 1. He is still an asshole. You have had enough of them to last you a lifetime, and 2. We work together, and I have had enough getting out of my last workplace romance. But the satisfaction of seeing his surprise when I pulled out my tools was worth every penny as I hid a smile behind my hair-tying distraction.

I also refuse to acknowledge that the fact that he was fixing the plane by himself is even more attractive to me than how tight his t-shirt was.

Another half hour passes as I finish most of the wiring for the actuator. It was just what I needed, some relaxing physical work, while I hum 90s songs.

As Jon wants to play the strong silent type today, I chose to be the grown-up in this exchange and start a less charged dialog before we either kill each other or... something else. I climb off the step stool, put my tools down and go around the plane to where Jon is lying on his back, focused on his landing gear. I could just sink on him displayed like that and it would be glorious, I think briefly, but realign myself.

"So, what exactly is the feud with Lex Aviation? By your reactions the other day, it seemed to be a bit more than just competition. Would really like to know what I am getting into here."

He stares at me from top to bottom slowly with those blazing green eyes that make me want to squirm under his glare, but I keep strong and start tapping my foot—that only makes him stare at my legs.

"Despite enjoying talking down to you, can you get up from there?" I ask before either of us derails the conversation again, ignoring the numerous techs in the surrounding hangar.

He is on his feet so fast, dropping the screwdriver, and again, I am shocked at how tall he is. I usually do not feel this tiny with my heels on, but this guy is towering over me every time, forcing me to look up at him, but I stop myself from cowering. He puts his arm on the wing, his T-shirt slightly running up his side, but stares over my head and around the enclosure, trying to delay whatever he wants to say. He starts rapping his fingers on the wing, so I guess he is anxious about whatever it is.

"She was a model and my dad's wife," he says abruptly, like a band-aid coming off.

"Umm, OK, that was absolutely not what I was expecting you to say," I admit in shock. "Without sounding totally anti-feminist, how does a model end up CEO of an aviation company—and a rival aviation company at that?"

He is thinking again, this time looking at me, assessing me like an opponent in chess.

"Deceit." Is his only answer and I see him getting worked up again, with possibly steam coming out of his ears.

"Riiight, I see the word count is getting lower by the second. Suspect only grunting will follow."

He only glares, proving me the bar was set too high.

"Two days," he snips at me instead.

"Have the fumes got to your head? What are you talking about?"

"Be in the office two days a week. I want to see progress reports weekly on the software. Also, I want to hear what your ex-husband may or may not want by working with Miranda."

I glare back.

Normally I would counter, but Jon seems to want to compromise, and I feel that probably I may give him one, despite his avoidance of telling me the full story with his nemesis.

"Fine, I'll be there on Tuesday. Now I really need to go as we almost had a normal conversation, so I think the sky will fall shortly."

As I move to collect my tools and put my glasses back in my purse, he just stays there, putting his head in his hands like he is at the end of his tether. For no reason I care to admit to myself, I turn to him and give a concession.

"The reason Richard is with Lex Aviation is probably the same as what you gave me about Miranda—he is a deceitful son of a bitch who has been lying to me for years. Based on your reactions, Miranda is pretty much on the same bandwidth so them together isn't good news. What I will do—seeing as you insist on dragging me into the office—is check your mainframe and see if anyone downloaded or sent anything suspicious."

He looks taken aback by my offer.

"You would do that?" he asks in shock, which makes me roll my eyes at him. "Thank you, that means a lot," Jon continues in a softer, heartfelt tone, which makes me go a bit soft myself. "They won't know what hit them, eh?" He chuckles and runs his fingers through his hair.

Him being playful makes me all gooey inside.

"Hey—I will not let them win now, am I?" I smile and he freezes.

"That is the first genuine smile I got from you," he says quietly, eyes ablaze with want. Everything between us is coming in like a tsunami, the attraction and the 'more' I didn't want to admit to my sister and definitely not to myself.

"Jon…" I start while not knowing how to end the sentence, but he takes the words I didn't want to say right out of my mouth.

"I know, I know, can't happen," he says, rapping his fingers again on the wing. "I will see you on Tuesday." He ducks, or more specifically sprints down under the plane, and the casual dismissal gives me an uncomfortable feeling I do not want to name.

I need to get out of there to regroup, maybe slap myself a couple of times for knowing damn well nothing should develop between us, but craving it just the same. I do not understand how just being near him confuses me so. Especially since half the time he is still so perplexing.

But as I walk towards the exit, I feel an absurd need to turn and when I do, he is looking at me and smiles. My dumb heart of mine causes me to grin too. One of the mechanics interrupts Jon to ask him something and I snap myself out of it, as despite what I was thinking last weekend, this can't go anywhere. I won't risk having my reputation affected again after how Richard played it at Hove.

I will go open Tinder and find myself a date for Saturday instead, as I really need to think about someone else.

JON

"Let me tell you, last weekend I got with the hottest girl—you wouldn't believe it! Legs for days, double Ds!" My best friend Nathan, as always, entertains me with too many details of his latest conquest.

"Yeah, yeah. Supermodel of the week, I hear you!" I nurse my lonely beer as I look around the bar on a busy Saturday night.

Didn't particularly want to come out but Nathan travels a lot so he isn't regularly free to go out and I decided I could use a distraction. Several women are checking us out, but I am not feeling it. Thoughts of the smile of a particular brunette are still fresh in my mind. And a tint of regret on how I acted like an oaf when she surprised me by asking about Miranda, poking at things I preferred not to get into with her so fast.

"Why is this bar so packed, man? I think half of Kerrington is trying to squeeze inside tonight. And lots of reporters, too," I comment, surveying the room.

"Well, it is the most popular place in town. As we always come here, I didn't even consider going anywhere else. It's pretty much our regular Saturday night when I am in. Ah, and Firebrand, you know, the rock band had a concert nearby, so many people went to that, and probably the press too. And now they are drinking. But enough about the fucking scenery, man. What happened to... what's her name? Sara? Simone?" Nathan inquires, taking a swig out of his beer.

"Sienna—nothing interesting, but that was pretty much it. The girl had the personality of a chair. Doesn't seem to take a hint though, kept texting—sometimes only emojis for fuck's sake—had to block her number."

"What's wrong with emojis?" he asks, confused. "Did you just say 'personality'? You want 'personality' now? A couple of years back, I couldn't find you under the mountain of pussy fighting over you. Look at you—rich, good-looking, what's the point of 'personality'?"

"Not everything is about sticking one's cock in, Nate. The more I go through these women, the more I realize it's more to living than just pussy. Though I admit, I have been known to take what's on offer." Again, I think of a fiery woman who jumped in my arms.

"Occasionally, I would like to have a conversation with them, maybe have a laugh," I continue. "All these faceless girls in my life... I mistakenly thought that Sienna was a bit more than she pretended, with her psychology degree and all that. It appears her daddy's money bought that paper, and all she psychoanalyzes is the latest 'Housewives of whatever' episode. Also, there is a lot going on at work nowadays—my EA is an idiot and Miranda started stealing my suppliers!" I vent.

"Jon, my man, from what I can hear, a woman is exactly what you need! I could also use a distraction, to be fair. But I have no interest in anything serious just now, you know I can't lose focus. Speaking of... do not turn—I call dibs! There is a total smoke show nursing a vodka tonic sitting by herself at a table out back! Shit—some dude sat down across from her... darn!"

I laugh at his antics, as he always finds himself someone for the night wherever he may be. Like me, he has his own business—producing playing cards and other commodities for casinos and card clubs. He has no intention of settling down due to reasons of his own, which I understand well, having known the man since high school. Ignoring his advice, I look to see who this stunner is, and when I spot who it is, I almost crush the glass in my hand.

Black leather skirt so tight, high heeled leather boots, a black top with an open back with a long necklace hanging down her spine. Dark hair done up on top of her head. Brown eyes whose burn I know too well. But what makes me really want to break my glass, or possibly that guy's face, is the fact that Dahlia Jara is on fucking DATE!

She is explaining something quite animatedly and the dude just sits there nodding his head, probably not understanding a word she says. Kind of good-looking but a bit plain, with chestnut hair, blue shirt and cheap shoes.

He seems to have gotten her a red rose, but as it lies there discarded on the table tells me she wasn't too impressed. Which makes me unintentionally pleased.

"Jon? Mate? What are you staring at, that chick I called dibs on? Hot right?" Nathan prompts from next to me.

"No dibs, I know her. You don't want to go there." I growl and turn back to my friend before I go over to her table and throw that guy out. The last thing I need is my friend getting interested in her with his easy smile, baby-blue eyes and panty-dropping Irish brogue.

"AAAAH, I see—where did you meet her? App?" He smirks, but is still gawking at her and is about five minutes from getting his eyeballs removed from his head.

"Work," I answer. "She works for me on a new software."

"Ah, so smart and sexy... so what is she doing with that tool? She doesn't seem that into him, frankly. You want to get in there? Suspect the dude will pee his pants and run if you just walk over." He shrugs.

"It's not like that. She's too irritating. And opinionated." I have been trying to convince myself. "Plus, I will repeat myself—she works for me!"

"I see. She's smart and sexy, understands your job and challenges you. Horrible combination." Nate shakes his head and looks at me strangely. "Well, in that case, you may not want to know she just touched her date's arm."

I turn so fast I almost spill my beer, but the man she was with is no longer there and I notice the woman heading towards the bar.

"Made you look! Man! I haven't seen you like this before. Hilarious! Anyway, I think I could use another drink. Shall I go get some?" he snickers, clearly implying something else. But I will not let my flighty friend tangle with... an employee of mine. NOT. AT. ALL.

"I'll go get them!" I declare and dash out of my chair before Nathan says another word and plans a path to the bar on the other side. I am convinced I can hear him laughing behind me but unsure of what he finds so amusing.

Making my way through the throng of people to order our drinks, I spot Dahlia trying to get the bartender's attention. Unfortunately, before I get there, I am intercepted by possibly the last person I want to run into.

"O.M.G! Something must be wrong with your phone, Jon! I have been texting you non-stop! I miss youuuu! I hoped you'd be here tonight. I came specifically for you!" My ex basically throws herself at me and I try to keep her off me. But it's harder than it should be with the crowd around the bar, so keeping the blonde off me is proving problematic.

"Sienna—we broke up. You need to stop texting me. Now, if you don't mind, I have to get to the bar." I try dodging her again, but she parks herself in front of me.

"Ha, we did not break up. You just needed a moment, but I am ready to take you back now!" She smiles like she is making any sense and pushes up her boobs, her warped mind driving her to think this will somehow persuade me that she isn't certifiable.

"OK, I don't think you understand me—we are O.V.E .R." If I spell it out for her maybe, she will finally get it.

An irritating laugh comes out of her, "Oh silly Jon, you are sooooo funny!" She tries again to touch me but I bat her hand away. I internally start cursing what life choices got me to this point when I hear a throaty siren voice next to me.

"Oh, honey," she purrs, "sorry it took so long. The bar was sooooo busy. Oh, and who are you? Do they let minors in nowadays?" Dahlia Jara slides her hand around my waist and throws a slightly unhinged smile at my ex.

Sienna squints at her shell-shocked, and then at me—who finally tweaked what is going on—putting my arm around Dahlia's back, feeling her silky skin against my hand. But the lunatic in front of us doesn't seem to get a hint and doubles down on her craziness.

"Jon, if you wanted a threesome, you could have just said. I have some old cheerleader friends I can call!"

I blank, speechless at that comeback, but then the woman I am holding starts laughing so hard I almost have to keep her upright. Not that I mind, that is. She is soft and warm and smells fantastic, of coconut and vanilla. She looks up at me with an evil grin.

"What do you think, honey? An orgy with some cheerleaders? Maybe they can bring their pom-poms?" She then turns her head to my former girlfriend, "But not you sweetie, you are not my type, with all the spray tan, all the chemicals are just a big no-no for me. I'll take your friend's phone number, though."

Then back at me in an exaggerated stage whisper, "Are there any male cheerleaders? I know how *you* appreciate a bit of variety," she adds, winking at me.

Sienna's face is now red as she finally realizes how outmatched she is.

"Fine—be like that, Jon! You'll regret this later. You could have had all of me!" The blonde huffs and tries to storm out, but the people are packed tightly as she has to battle her way out in defeat, making the whole escape quite anticlimactic. Unfortunately, as soon as she is out of sight, Dahlia moves away from me, and I immediately feel the loss, but I manage to put my hands in my pockets.

"A bit of variety?" I ask in a low voice.

"Well, I think the words you are looking for are 'why, thank you DJ for saving me from my future child bride. I really appreciate avoiding my destiny of listening to Korean boy bands and hearing about the latest TikTok videos or something along those lines." She crosses her arms and raises an eyebrow at me.

"Thanks," I say through my teeth, but deep down I am in awe of her quick thinking and admire the fact that she came to help me. Just as I am about to tell her that, my ill-timed companion crashes our conversation.

"Hello, hello. Who do we have here—that was an epic takedown! Heard the whole thing! Should have recorded it really! I am Nathan, this idiot's better looking best friend... and you—gorgeous warrior princess, you are?" He almost bats his eyelashes as he turns on his 1000-watt smile. With his fitted navy shirt, rolled cuffs and strong build, I am about to send him packing, far, far away from her.

She looks at me and deadpans, "DJ, I work with the idiot." And towards my mate—she is fucking smiling at him! "Very not interested, Nathan. But love the warrior princess line though, solid 7 out of 10!"

Nate giggles like a teenager before saying, "Ah, my heart is broken forever! I was about to drag this bonehead to a club... Do you want to join us? I would like to hear how to increase my score with you!"

I mumble something along the lines of "There will be no scoring tonight," but DJ answers with an eye roll.

"Yeah, I think I will just be heading out. Nothing good will come out of me going clubbing. Have a good evening, guys!" she closes the conversation curtly and then darts towards the door.

"We'll walk you to your taxi!" I intervene and grab Nathan by the arm to catch DJ before she goes out into a dark car park at night dressed in that outfit. Her necklace moves with her back as she waves through the crowd, her ass looking fantastic in that leather skirt. I have to elbow my friend as I spot him checking her out, which makes him grin.

As we approach the exit, Nate pushes me forward. "You go—I think I forgot... something at our table." He winks at me and mouths a 'go get her' which gains him a middle finger from me, and an 'asshole' mouthed back.

Fucking asshole, leaving me like that.

I get out the door into the carpark looking for the maddening woman. However, I immediately lose my train of thought as DJ is a few yards away and is pushing a guy off her.

"Back off!" she shouts and bats his arm away, as an older man dressed in jeans and a black shirt shoves a phone close to her face.

I get there instantly and drag her behind me, though she squirms trying to get to him herself. I growl at the dude, prepared to put him down if necessary. "You better move several steps back NOW!"

"Jeez, it's Jon McMaster, the actual CEO! It's just my night!" The guy is absolutely giddy, which makes me glance at Dahlia, who seems to be fuming, holding on to my shirt but ready to deck the man. "Kev Greer from the 'Observer'," he continues. "Do you have a comment for the press on why you hired a convicted felon in your IT department?"

DJ

I just had to get out of there. Intervening was a mistake. Touching him was an even bigger one. Of course, I spotted them in the corner by the window as I sat down at my table to wait for my date.

Tall, broad-shouldered, dressed in black jeans and a black shirt, sleeves rolled up and his stupidly expensive watch on display with his sculpted forearms and sexy tattoos. A mane of light brown hair attracting every singleton in the bar like a cliché moth to the flame. My date—whose name I do not recall—was a nice pediatrician who got me a nice rose and tried to make nice conversation. Though him probably picking the busiest place in town was not the best idea. I struggled to forget about Jon as I attempted to explain my job, but frankly, nothing else was in my mind than the Man in the corner. So, I told him I didn't want to waste his time and left for the bar to get another drink when I heard the obnoxious screech of his ex-girlfriend's voice.

Somehow, seeing plastic-is-fantastic Barbie throwing herself at him, I thought to myself to go and 'save' him, as he was ridiculously trying to hold her off, akin to a bear fighting a monkey.

Then he put his massive arm around me and held me when I burst into laughter at his childish ex's antics, and all years of being a strong independent 'can stand on my own two feet and I don't need a man' bullshit went out the window. All I wanted was to not step out of his embrace, surrounded by that manly scent which I appreciate even more after seeing him in the hangar yesterday. But that is why I had to move when the ankle biter left with her tail between her legs. Luckily, his cheesy friend also provided some respite so I could escape.

Pushing my body as fast as I can towards the taxi stand trying to avoid them, and all of a sudden, a phone is in my face and a short guy is talking a million words a minute.

"Dahlia Jara! I work for the Observer! How did you get a job with McAv aviation with your criminal record? Does your employer know you are a violent offender?"

I only manage an angry 'back off!' and a push, when a giant shadow appears between me and the reporter I was about to pummel and thrusts me backward, in a clear protective move which I am not used to, but makes something flutter inside me.

"Jeez, it's Jon McMaster, the actual CEO! It's just my night!" The guy is delighted, and I am bordering on actually becoming a violent offender. "Kev Greer from the

'Observer'," he introduces himself. "Do you have a comment for the press on why you hired a convicted felon in your IT department?"

I can feel Jon stiffening in front of me as I clutch his shirt harder and want to say something to explain the total bullshit the guy is spurring. Then, suddenly, he yanks the man's phone from his hand, lifts it high as the reporter tries to take it back but does not have the reach of my caveman. He goes into the apps deleting whatever was recorded, and he throws the guy's phone a few feet toward an alley.

Jon thunders a "No comment," then takes my hand in his massive one and starts dragging me after him. All I can do is follow him, leaving the reporter scrambling to find his device.

As I try to keep up with his long strides through the carpark, he abruptly stops in front of a large SUV, opens the passenger door and picks me up like I weigh nothing and almost throws me inside, closing the door. As he goes around to the driver's side, gets in, then takes a lengthy breath and runs his hands through his hair.

"Jon, it's not what you think. He was lying," I begin, as he deserves an explanation, but I get a 'shh'. He pulls out his own phone and starts a call, looking straight out the windscreen.

"Julia, how are you? Sorry for calling so late. I hear someone, a guy called Kev Greer, is trying to pass some false information as news on your paper. Can you please look into it for me? Perhaps talk to the other media owners here. Wouldn't want to upset our advertising contract with your company now, would we?" The last phrase is more of a rumble which goes straight between my legs, as apparently, I find low-voiced threats extremely exciting. "Yes, of course McAv will be at your charity luncheon next Saturday. We definitely support our local community and wildlife. OK, I'll leave you to enjoy your evening, Julia, speak later in the week."

The call ended, his knuckles white gripping the device, then another long breath, and the phone gets put down on the console. I am the recipient of a blast of green eyes, and a shiver of excitement goes down my back.

"Well, feel free to start," he says quietly.

I stare at my hands in my lap for a moment, as I never thought this would be a conversation I would have any time soon with a guy I had sex with. Especially not in a dark carpark after getting basically attacked by a reporter. I know Jon needs an explanation as without his connections here in Florida, that article could have hurt both me and his company, but as I start speaking, I lose it a bit.

"Obviously, I am going to begin by confirming I am NOT a convicted felon! Or a violent criminal or an offender!" I do not even notice I am talking with my hands and basically hyperventilating until he takes my hand in his and squeezes me gently.

"I know DJ, never believed that for a second," he tells me tenderly, and I feel my eyes tearing up, but I blink quickly to hide it.

He opens the console fridge, passing me a water and getting one for himself. I take a few drinks and put the bottle down. Before I start the story I never wanted to repeat, Jon takes my hand again, his fingers intertwining with mine, and somehow, it strikes me as the most natural feeling in the world.

"As Hove's route software was beginning to take off a few years back, I was out with some folk from work and my best friend at that time, Janine. On that evening I met Richard—hot, charming, smart—son of a congressman, but he didn't seem to act entitled or anything. He was also at Hove, in Purchasing actually, so we knew a lot of the same people. We started going out, and we had lots of fun, as it was all easy, nothing very serious. Fast forward a few months, and somehow, one night, we had a bit too much to drink. But having too much to drink in Vegas had the very unintentional consequence of a ring on my finger in the morning, and social media full of pictures from our wedding."

"What? You got married by an Elvis impersonator?" The disbelief on Jon's face is apparent.

"Don't be daft. It was a Dolly Parton impersonator," I huff with a smile.

At that obviously, Jon starts laughing so I have to mock-punch him in the arm.

"Come on, don't be like that—I was wasted! Somehow Richard managed to convince me not to get an annulment right away. He pleaded with me, as it would have looked bad for his father who was running for the Senate—again, social media posts are a very silly idea—and we agreed to 'give it a go'. Anyway... as you can imagine, after a few more months the marriage wasn't going so great, but I was so busy with Hove's maintenance and started 'Zephyr' that frankly I couldn't be bothered to try to fix it. I was coding 16-hour days mostly and barely saw him for weeks on end. I know I should have ended it then and there, but I honestly didn't care that much either way. But what surprised me was that one day out of the blue he decided he wanted to 'make it work'—couples councilors, all that jazz."

"Then he started being interested in 'Zephyr'." I sigh. "That should really have raised some alarm bells as, despite him being a computer science student like myself, he is far more focused on business and politics than coding—which is probably why he never got his degree. But I thought little about it at the time and explained my premise and the code structure in broad lines to him."

"The information you gave him persuaded the judge that he was involved in the work you were doing?" The clever man next to me shakes his head gently.

"Yes, part of the reasoning. It gets worse." I continue staring out into the dark car park, then take a risk asking. "You feel like driving? I am a bit claustrophobic staying here stationary."

"I love to drive, actually; my driver takes me when I need to the office, but I could really go for a drive right about now as well. I'll drop you off while you tell me more of your tale of woe."

"Woe? Again with the words! Do you have a 'word of the day' calendar?"

He rolls his eyes at me while I smirk and add, "I am at 156 Grove Lane. This isn't how I imagined this evening going in the slightest... but thank you for being my Uber."

Putting the car in 'D', Jon chuckles at me, "Yes, a lot of unexpected events happen with you around."

I turn my head towards the side window, so he doesn't see me blush and decide I might as well put it all on the table.

"One day I had an excellent idea on getting data from some private satellites for the weather patterns and of all ridiculous things that could have happened—my third computer screen packed it in at home. So, I decided that going into the office would be a great plan. I cannot only work on two screens anymore, of course. What was not a great plan was stopping by to say 'hello' to my friend—and Marketing manager at Hove—Janine."

"Ah, I can see where this is leading to," Jon says quietly, and I should have known as well.

The lights of Kerrington were passing us by, Jon's car swaying from lane to lane, taking the long way to my house, passing the beach, and then the business district.

"Yes, it was 'going' exactly how you expect, on her glass desk. Richard had a moment of shock to see me there. Janine—the bitch—didn't even feign remorse. I stormed out and then I did something really stupid."

"This should be good—suspect you didn't stop at throwing away his stamp collection or shrinking his clothes?"

"Mmm, that would have been a wonderful idea, but I think you noticed I have a bit of a temper."

"Yes," he clips, "you are a bit tempestuous." He gives me a pointed look before I pounce on another of his posh phrases.

I roll my eyes at the big word and then confess what another night of tequila bought. My fingers dig into the black leather of the car seat, bracing for my confession.

"Well, I went home... had a few too many drinks—I really can't handle tequila—and... I'll just say it in one, judge me at your leisure... I-slashed-his-tires-and-carved-ASS-HOLE-into-his-hood!"

I put my head in my hands and low-key scream.

Jon looks at me, stunned, just as he pulls the car over in front of my driveway. I peek through my fingers at him.

"Come on—say something," I prod, really wanting to know what he thinks.

"Let me get this straight." He runs his fingers through his hair, finding his words. "You... Carrie Underwood-ed him?"

Those were not the words I thought he would say, but they were exactly what I needed, and that puts a shy smile on my face.

"Yes, I have indeed Carrie Underwood-ed him, though she sang about a slightly different revenge," I comment and take a deep breath. "In case you were wondering, I did not get convicted as it was my name on the car deed—I give great presents. I didn't even spend a night in jail either, not even a mug shot—to my sister's disappointment. The police were quite understanding, but it was absolutely mortifying."

The silence in the SUV is oppressive as he just stares out the window. I am thinking I should probably get out of there when, out of nowhere, Jon starts snickering. Then he gets louder and louder as he is on a full-on belly laugh.

That loud, warming laugh I have been avoiding admitting I have been longing to hear again ever since that day at Marcus's shop.

"Oh, my gosh! Stop laughing! It was really embarrassing with the police at my door! The look on their faces! When I showed them the pink slip of the car, they just stared at me with some very judgemental looks and left."

But he doesn't stop. I don't think he can stop and then I start giggling as well, then I can't check myself either and burst into laughter as well. Just like that, we are two idiots laughing in a car on a Saturday night.

And it feels... right.

I feel... wonderful.

As our fit of laughter dies down eventually, we end up staring at each other across the console and then the silence morphs. From oppression into intensity. Intensity into heat. Heat into connection.

Jon moves first, gently taking my face in his large hands, running his thumb over my lower lip, and looking at me like I am Christmas morning. I do not dare breathe as I stare into his green eyes, wanting him more than I wanted anything. The first touch of his lips on mine is light, almost worshiping me. Like he craves to savor this moment of peace between us, of quiet and reverence.

Again and again, he kisses me softly, lips only, my face still cradled just how he wants me, tasting me. Minutes or years go by. Just feeling his mouth on mine, his soft beard against my skin, the heat of his hands on my face, the wetness between my legs from just these chaste kisses. Only when I run my fingers through his soft wavy hair, pulling him closer to me as much as the console between us allows, do I feel his tongue demanding entry to my mouth.

I part my lips and then, with a low rumble through his chest, he starts properly kissing me. His tongue dances with mine as he angles my head for better access. Wishing there was no boundary between us, my tongue delves in, exploring his mouth, as he does mine. The only sounds in the car are of our pants and moans as we kiss and kiss, not touching more than our faces, but even just this—it is just glorious. It's falling off an edge or reaching the peak of a mountain. Full of danger and promise and wonder and hotter than any kiss I ever had or probably ever will have.

Jon breaks away first, his forehead resting on mine. I am gasping, drunk on the feeling of his lips. His breathing is erratic as well and for a moment we just stay frozen, woozy, intoxicated on each other.

"I shouldn't have done that," he whispers, fracturing the magic. "You work for me—I can't do this." Abruptly, and leaving me reeling, he gets out of the car and comes and opens my door.

I manage to get out, unable to fully understand what is happening as my brain is mush.

"Jon—I am confused." Understatement of the year.

"I'm sorry," he apologizes for the wrong reason. "I need to go now before I throw you over my shoulder and drag you inside."

My vagina thinks that sounds pretty great but before I manage to verbalize it, my caveman wraps the back of my neck with his big hand and kisses me again.

Jon mumbles, "Last time," as he conquers me with his punishing touch and holds me like wants to brand me.

I am weak in the knees when he leaves me disoriented in front of my house as he gets back in his Range Rover. I press on my lips as he looks at me longingly, but then restarts the car and drives off, and all I think is 'what the fuck'.

I get a second 'what the fuck' moment later in the night, tossing and turning in my bed trying to quench a need no vibrator can fix when I realize—I thought of him as 'my' caveman.

DJ

Tuesday morning, I didn't go to say 'hello' to Jon, the infuriating, maddening hunk. If the annoying jerk thinks he can just leave me literally soaked on my driveway and then run away, he has another thing coming to him. I head straight into the IT office downstairs and close the door, continuing to recover my software, but mostly banging my fingers on the keyboard and not thinking about him at all. Not at all.

***

Marcus and Laura made fun of me Sunday at lunch, as I was still fuming.

"So, what got your panties in a twist? Or shall I say... who?" My younger sibling was inclined to needle me.

"How about you mind your own business before I tell mamá you don't want to go out with her friend Marisol's niece?" I countered, knowing my brother's disdain for getting arm-twisted into going on set-ups. My mom wants to find us all partners, but after Laura's husband's death and my divorce, her only target is poor Marcus. Obviously, every tía seems to know a 'nice girl' willing to date him.

"Ooof," he laughed. "I see someone is bringing out the big guns! I may tell her myself—I am so tired of all the awkward dates, really. Seriously now, are you OK?"

"Yes," I lied, "just fucking great. I don't want to generalize, but most men truly are idiots, aren't they?"

"I can't disagree, but suspect idiocy in relationships applies to all genders." Marcus sighed and poured us both some more wine.

Laura came outside, glanced at us chugging fermented grape juice, and got a glass for herself. "So, are we drinking or are we Drinking? Is this the man from the other week—the one who you lunched on in the store?"

I could see Marcus's face turning green. "You did what in my shop?"

"I admit nothing." Not to Marcus. He would have rubbed it in, his older sister debasing his workplace.

"Jeez DJ, I thought you just flirted with the dude! How am I the least strumpet-y of all of us?"

Lau and I shook our heads, as Marcus wasn't exactly a catholic priest when it comes to getting some. Just a bit of a prima donna when he can poke at one of us.

"Probably because you can't get a date without mom playing Cupid," my sister goaded him, knowing he doesn't need the help. "So, what if DJ got a man snack? What happened? Did you see him again? Thought you were on a date yesterday with a doctor?"

"I was indeed. But before I talk about last night, I must tell you something."

They stared at me.

"Well... are you telling us or what?" Marcus asked with impatience.

"My meeting with McAv, the ones I told you I got the contract with. Their CEO... Jon McMaster... is the GUY from the store."

It is Laura who spoke first, with a shit-eating grin on her face, as my brother was still in shock.

"I bet you got that contract, wink wink! Just kidding sis', I know you are outstanding. They would have been stupid not to sign with you. So is the reason you are in a 'feed me wine' mood today because you can't ride his magic cock anymore if you work together?"

"Jeez Lau, can you not say the words 'ride' and 'cock'?" Marcus blushing like a nun every time we use sex phrases is one of our favorite pastimes.

"Pretty much why I was angry earlier in the week. I can't get into it with another guy at the job after Richard bad mouthed me at Hove and basically made me quit. The reason I am fuming today, however, is that I accidentally saw him at the bar I was in yesterday."

"When you were on that Tinder date? Wow, Telenovela much?" Laura snickered as she refilled her wine glass, nodding at me to continue.

"Yep, the guy was not that exciting and anyway... I ran into Jon and his friend, and he ended up giving me a lift. We had a bit of a conversation in the car..." I didn't want to tell my family about the reporter. Laura had t-shirts made up with 'orange is the new black' when she heard about the police incident in California. I also didn't want to admit to losing my shit to them, and I am still a tad embarrassed by that.

"And you ended up christening his back seat!" she whooped.

"No, we didn't re-enact your high school nights, you hussy." I rolled my eyes at her. "We made out like the world was ending though, but then he goddamn stopped, telling me we can't do this as I work for him. Then the pendejo runs off, leaving me in my driveway!" I exploded, also chugging my wine and start opening a fresh bottle.

"Wait... didn't you just tell us you can't get on with him because you work with him? Why are you worked up now?" our male sibling asked, confused.

"Oh, sweet child of summer..." Laura tried to pat his head, and he batted her hand away. "She can claim all she wants that she can't get on with him—Richard needs another whack for that—but it doesn't mean she doesn't WANT to climb him like a jungle gym. Right, lil D? Based on the French-and-dash session, I suspect he has the same conundrum."

"I can't answer what his issue is, but he kissed me this time and then he ran off."

"OK hermana. We are definitely Drinking today, but tomorrow you need to start figuring out if you can drop the 'we work together' act and try to see if there is something there. You, sis, don't take the first 'no' for an answer when you want something. At least you should talk to him and clear the air." My younger brother is somehow the calm one between us. Me and my sister are more alike, but Marcus is often the peacemaker in the family. He was right this time.

There were quite a few bottles of wine emptied on Sunday between the three of us, with my mamá and my uncle Antonio looking at us like aliens. Monday—let's just say working from home was the best idea I ever had, between my headache and not admitting I don't want to face Jon in the office. Or maybe I wanted to grab him from the lapels of this jacket and shake him.

***

I continue thinking as well why would Jon keep saying I work for him? But I suppose I need to put on my big girl pants and talk to him. Which implies actually 'woman-up'-ing not just hiding in the basement.

My stomach growls around lunchtime, but I am close to repairing the wind speed section of the code and don't pay attention to the door opening until I jump in my seat, hearing a high-pitched voice.

"Hi Dahlia!" Mike Jones walks into my den and brings me a cupcake. "Here is a 'Welcome to the office' treat!" The jolliness continues as though we are in a bad sitcom.

"Thanks," I say and look at her, waiting for the actual reason she stopped by, strongly suspecting it has a lot to do with a certain Thor lookalike.

"Just wanted to see how you are settling in... I know the IT department is a bit... dark," she comments, looking around, cringing. "I thought you would be upstairs in one of the touch-down areas—you don't need to stay here. We got desks next to windows, too."

It is literally a murky cave basement, with a few desks with triple screens, a sofa and a table with mismatched chairs, probably the ones left over from the past couple of office refurbs. The walls have science fiction movie posters and some rude comments written in marker all over them, and the fridge contains mostly energy drinks and chocolate, only slightly out of date.

I

Fucking

Love it!

—but will never admit it. Maybe I will bring my team in some time. They will love it here as well. Maybe we can do a little DOTA Lan-party.

"Yes, it is a tad gloomy but helps me focus," I respond neutrally. "Can I help you with anything else?"

"If you could, there is a little thing—Jon reminded me we need to represent the company at the Observer's charity luncheon this Saturday. You know, the money goes to local wildlife and there will be a lot of press and lots of nearby companies will send representatives."

I look at Michaela's lively demeanor—and think this lady is pretty slick, cheerful façade and all. She is definitely rocking that metallic silver pantsuit she has on.

"So I hear," I deadpan. "Is there a question somewhere in there?"

"I was wondering if you would like to take my place. I am throwing my son a party for his return from New York—he finished his Master's at Columbia after transferring over from Boulder." She ignores my attempt at needling her and continues her happy-go-lucky attitude.

86

"Me? What does Mr. McMaster think about me coming along?" I counter, raising an eyebrow as we both know Jon doesn't have a clue I am being asked to attend.

"Probably it's best we don't tell him. Normally, he wouldn't need any support to shake hands with local CEOs and press. But the reason I want you to go is that you can handle him, and knowing that Miranda will be there, he needs backup—and someone to drag him back from possible murder."

"Handle him? I am not sure if he can handle ME!" I add, but I purse my lips and ponder about the offer.

Hearing Miranda will attend makes me think that Richard will show as he can't stop himself from kissing ass at events. Unbalancing the son of a bitch—and another foolish man I know—strikes me as a fan-freaking-tastic way of spending my Saturday. I definitely want to go. However, before I accept, I take the opportunity to ask a few questions of my own. The 'Man of the day' had too few words to say regarding his history with Lex Aviation and what I see as more personal reasoning, his grudge against his rival.

"You have been here at McAv for a while?" I start by making some polite conversation to not spook Ms. Jones here.

"Oh, I have been working here for like 30 years! I was Dave's secretary—as was the job name back then, none of this executive assistant mumbo jumbo. Jon's father saw something more in me and I got a chance to work with contracts. Slowly, I got promoted to this VP position about 17 years ago, unfortunately just a couple of years later, Dave passed away." She sighs and all I can think is—has this lady been a Vice president for that long?

But then it occurs to me she is essentially Jon's second in command and there is nowhere else up for her to go and seems to be quite contended in her position.

"That is a long time in the company."

"Ah, this business is basically my life! I do not imagine working anywhere else. I know every nook and cranny! Oh, Dahlia—the stories I could tell!" She winks at me between the ohs and the ahs.

"I could definitely listen to a specific story—Miranda Lexington." I narrow my eyes at her.

Mike blanches a bit, all cheeriness gone, then sits down and looks behind her back as if we are in a spy movie.

"Not sure how much Jon told you, I'd rather not gossip," she whispers, continuing the 'cloak and dagger' vibe. But I wasn't born yesterday either—she yearns to chitchat but needs some sort of permission, it seems.

"He mentioned me she was married to his father," I match her hushed voice, but do not explain that is all I know from the grunting bear.

"Oh, OK you know that!" The relief in her voice is clear. "Well, they were married for about a year and a bit before Dave passed away. I believed she was not in the will, but she got off with a few million. As it appears, Dave changed his will last minute to include her. Jon got the company. She left with all that money, then she met another billionaire—Ramsay Lexington. From what I hear, she persuaded him to go into aviation and he named her CEO! She still has some sort of grudge against her former stepson, and she has been spending a lot of time and energy trying to steal our contracts and suppliers."

That clarifies a bit why Jon hates her, as I suspect he was also not expecting his father's trophy wife to get that much money.

"So, have you been by his side since he took over? Was he also a VP when his dad passed?"

"Jon? Lord no! He had no interest in McAv. Well, more than tinkering with those planes in the hangar—he spent his youth gallivanting through Europe, doing extreme sports and whatnot. I think he was shocked to get the company, but his father always thought he was his heir."

"Hmm," I grunt, as I sense something here. "Did Miranda expect to inherit the firm? McAv is worth billions."

The silver-haired woman is quiet for a bit, eyes moving away from me. If we had a working window down here, I suspect she would have looked out through it, avoiding the answer.

"Who is to say what she was expecting? Maybe she thought she was Dave's favorite, and seeing Jon inherit it all made her... upset," she dodges, checking her nails. "Anyway, enough history lessons. Can I count on you to attend the luncheon?"

"I will be there, don't worry," I confirm out loud the decision I made 10 minutes ago, but I can see there is more to the story which makes me want to go to the event even more.

As Ms. Jones finally leaves, I decide to resume the checks on the network I promised McAv's CEO in the hangar the other week.

I also need to decide for myself whether I want more with Jon.

JON

The charity event is already hell on earth, and I have only been there for 20 minutes. Julia Li adores the glamor of hosting these parties but somehow thinks we all enjoy them. Or just loves torturing all of us by making us all show up. The venue is by the boardwalk, with big windows on one side overlooking the sea, and luckily the air conditioning is at full blast and Florida's heat is kept at bay.

I am at my second drink already—non-alcoholic as well as I had the brilliant idea to drive myself. I ponder escaping another handshake with a local celebrity or some more small talk with some councilor wanting us to make some other extension or open additional facilities so they can claim they bring jobs to Kerrington.

You'd think that having a major aviation company in town would give me a break, but all these politicians want is to bleed me dry and make themselves look good.

It doesn't help that I have been reflecting on the events of last Saturday all week, and of a certain employee of mine I shouldn't be thinking of. One I most definitely shouldn't have mauled in my car. One who shouldn't be giving me a hard-on by reminiscing about the taste of her lips, wanting to pound her tight pussy into the next century. An employee who makes me angry and happy and annoys me to no end. I smile to myself, imagining her slashing tires with 'Before he cheats' blasting through the speakers.

One who most certainly shouldn't be walking into this restaurant dressed in a yellow dress, with a sleeveless top and a flowy skirt flaring from her hips, ending halfway down her thigh, highlighting her long legs in some high heeled strappy sandals. The dress is cropped to the sides, showing her delicious bronze skin and her soft hair is floating down her back. She looks as a wet dream with smoky eyes and nude lipstick. A summer dream turning into a thunderstorm the moment she spots me. I can feel her anger radiating in waves toward me as she approaches, and before being razed off the face of the earth by DJ's wrath, our host intercepts her.

"Oh my, you are Dahlia Jara! Welcome to Florida! I am Julia Li—absolutely delighted to meet you! Jon, you didn't say you have a superstar joining us."

"Didn't I?" I say through my teeth. "Must have forgotten with all the focus on the local wildlife."

DJ throws me a look that could melt steel but pastes on a smile for Julia.

"Julia, so nice to make your acquaintance! I have heard such good things about you and this charity. Is it the sea turtle or the key deer you are promoting today?" and turning her gaze towards me, attempting to turn me to stone, she continues, "or perhaps the Key Largo... woodrat?"

The Observer's owner seems slightly stumped to answer exactly what local wildlife she is asking for money for, which I find extremely amusing, despite the clear 'woodrat' jab aimed at me.

"Umm, we support several endangered species—uh, is that Mitch from the Miami Dolphins? I really must say 'hello'!" Ms. Li excuses herself before she gets asked more uncomfortable questions such as how the funds will be distributed, which I now realize I need to get more information on.

"That was interesting. I must ask my PI to investigate this charity a bit," I murmur for only DJ's ears, and my comment seems to interest her, the fury diminishing.

"You have a PI? Have they checked your company's email traffic? Do they check bags on people at the end of the day?" She goes off on a tangent, but at least the fires of Doom have been quelled.

"That is strangely specific—but yes, they had a look, no obvious emails with 'secret files' as the subject was sent to Lex Aviation if that's what you are asking. We even have an AI firewall running, trying to flag all suspicious traffic. It would be very difficult for anyone to send information using company laptops or phones. Also, we ask everyone to get their smartphones cameras covered by a very-hard-to remove sticker or to leave their personal devices in lockers at the entrance—with call diverting, of course, in case of emergencies. It is a bit 'prison style' but with what has been going on, people understand, and it's only temporary," I explain.

"We always checked bags by lottery for parts and tools missing, but since we lost the tire supplier, I also asked the security team to go through all bags and any paperwork exiting the site. Everyone's managers need to sign off on any documents or components taken out physically. Again, we can't check on everyone, but usually the threat of getting caught is quite a deterrent. Why do you ask?"

Holding her vodka tonic, she says, "I have been checking your network and you are right, nothing out of the ordinary with your emails. I even cast a glance at your bills, and while most of them went way over my head, I was shocked at your landline bill, but you have a lot of employees. Some really long phone calls there, however, suspect some are describing their weekend."

She is sitting close to me for our hushed conversation and her coconutty scent with undertones of vanilla invades my nostrils. I want to touch her again, taste her all over. I have to say something to not give away how distracted I am by her.

"Yes, a lot of employees talking personal stuff, you should see the number of memes that get sent." I don't do the best job at redirecting, as from this angle I gaze upon her delicate neck and traces of her cleavage as she looks past my shoulder, surveying the room.

When she touches my arm, I feel the warmth of her hand through my shirt and jacket.

"We need to talk about last Saturday," she changes the subject, surprising me with the direct opening. The room appears to quiet around us, as her palm touches my arm and flaming brown eyes meet my own. But then DJ brusquely pulls away, not before poking me in the chest again with her finger. "And we will talk Jon, just after I make sure this girl is OK."

She beelines for the toilets as I notice the silhouette of a young brown-haired girl in a green dress, running towards the Ladies, clearly crying. My heart stops as I recognize her instantly, even though I haven't seen her outside a video call in months. I dart after them, only to get a door shut in my face.

DJ

I may have been ready to tear Jon a new one after running away last Saturday, but upon reflection, I could have gone to his office this week to confront him, so there was more than one coward here.

Looking at him from a distance talking to some guests at the event, dressed in a casual white suit, with a navy pin-stripe shirt, white collar and matching blue pocket square, my pulse quickens. Especially seeing him easily laughing and wooing the surrounding people, making them raptly follow whatever it is he's saying, his confidence addictive.

So, after doing some breathing exercises, I decided to go over there and have a conversation like adults, though I had some unresolved anger lingering.

But seeing that young girl running away in distress, I put my caveman on the back burner and followed her in, shutting the door for some privacy.

"Hey are you OK?" I ask gently as I sit next to her on the couch in the marble clad restroom.

"Yes, thank you," she says between sobs. "You wouldn't happen to have a tissue?"

I pass her one from a pack on the counter, but as she continues crying, I give her the whole box.

"You want to talk about it? I can go punch whoever upset you if you wish. Maybe a Manolo to their shin? What do you think?"

"Oh no, that won't be necessary." She stops sniveling a bit. "You are very pretty," she adds, taking in my outfit and way too-expensive haircut. A pair of bright green eyes stare at me behind a lovely, freckled face. She has curly brown hair resembling a halo around her head, and her brown skin contrasts beautifully with her green smock.

"Thank you very much. You are very beautiful as well."

"Uh, I do not know about that," she retreats behind a tissue, looking defeated, making me angry.

"Damn right you are pretty! Let's not even mention this dress! It's great on you. If you weren't a teenager, I would say it looks hot on you!"

She smiles at me now, but then asks me a question which makes me go from 1 to 100 on the furious scale.

"It's just... I know I probably shouldn't ask you this, but... do you think I am fat?"

Staring at her trying to answer her unexpected question without exploding, I can see a healthy-looking girl about 13 or 14 years old. She is absolutely at normal weight for her age, in my view.

"Fat? What do you mean? Is that why you were crying? Look at me—what is your name?"

"Tabitha, but people sometimes call me Tae."

"Tae—I am DJ—and you are most definitely not fat. Whoever makes you feel you need to be thinner is about to get my heel shoved deeply up their ass."

At that she giggles, and I realize my swearing is probably not appropriate for children, but in this case, I think it is more than needed.

"It's just that..." she continues softly, "all my friends are skinnier than me. Also, I have started getting these stretch marks on my hips. I am ugly."

"Pfft stretch marks! Ha, I have those too—look!" I take advantage of my cropped dress to show her some of the skin around my sides, which she surveys clinically. "I even get a chin hair or two sometimes! Don't get me started on the occasional zit that flares up before my period!"

"You do? But you are so lovely," she says, slightly blushing.

"Thank you, Tae, but you need a better mirror. With those eyes and irresistible curls on you, I suspect the boys—or girls—will be falling over themselves for you in a couple of years."

"You think?" her voice grows in confidence a bit.

"I am positive. People don't mind normal skin. I know for a fact that the hottest man I've ever seen is into me, and some stretch marks and a bit of orange peel skin didn't stop him from kissing me silly." And other things I probably do not want to get into with a young lady in a bathroom.

Tabitha giggles again and, as simple as that, the mood lifts.

"That is what my brother says all the time. That I am beautiful, and the mean girls at school can go... fork... themselves. He tries not to swear around me. He is just a bit of a big dork, honestly—he reads books about elves and all." Then she switches directions to me. "You really have a hot boyfriend?"

"Umm, he isn't actually my boyfriend as... you know—gotta keep them guessing," I fib a bit for dramatic effect. "But your brother seems like a smart guy—you should listen to him. And seriously, why were you crying today? Are your friends here trying to make you feel bad?"

"Oh, I had a second piece of cake," her voice goes quiet again.

"OK... what is wrong with that?" I ask, quite confused. "I had three, and they were delicious."

"Umm, my mom said I need to pace myself if I still want to fit in this dress by the end of the day."

A loud thud shakes the chandelier in the restroom as the door hits the wall and a raging Jon roars, "SHE SAID WHAT?"

Before I get up to throw him out for scaring the girl to death with his yelling, Tabitha runs into his arms and starts crying again.

"Jon, I can't believe you are really here!" She bawls all over his shirt as he bear-hugs her.

"It's OK Tae, I am here," he soothes her and rubs his hands on her back. "Now what did Miranda say? I am going to have a talk with her."

"No! Don't!" the teenager shrieks. "I don't want you two fighting. You know she doesn't want me to keep in contact with you—she'll just get mad and take my phone away again."

"Look..." Jon sits her back down on the couch and lowers on one knee in front of her on the bathroom tiles, white pants and all. "She should not be saying things like that to you. There is nothing wrong with having cake, and as I always say, you are the most beautiful girl ever. Now come on, let's get your face washed and let's get you back to the party."

Tae's green eyes match Jon's, and I realize who the dorky—yet supportive—brother is. And who her mother is. My heart goes thumping in my chest seeing him in that position, so different from his asshole CEO image. However, the young woman throws me a 'help me' look, probably at the thought of having her bro next to her when using the toilet.

"Come on Jon, us ladies will put on our war face, you can wait outside." I push him gently up and out the door. "We will be just fine, but some of the charity Stepford wives won't take kindly to you looming in the Ladies' restroom. You may even get a 'bless your heart'," I smile at him.

I wasn't expecting it, but before closing the door again, Jon pulls me closer to him and whispers in my ear, his breath against my skin warming me up, "Thank you for this, DJ. I truly appreciate it."

"I would not let her cry by herself in the bathroom, for fuck's sake. I am ecstatic that now I have a target for my

Manolo's now," I whisper back and he chuckles, his beard slightly tickling my face and sending wake-up signals to my vajayjay.

"Well, I hear you are also familiar with the hottest guy in the world," he hisses, his lips lightly graze my ear, and goose bumps erupt all over my back and arm.

"What *I* know is that people eavesdropping need to mind their own business and check their presumptions. As their ego doesn't need stroking," I mention casually but raise the stakes by gently nipping his neck. Then, I shove him out in the hallway and say loud enough for his sister to hear.

"Right, big brother, time for you to shoo, I got this, thanks for the assist." I wink and shut the door in his face again, but this time on the sound of his laughter.

"Now Tabitha, how about a nice boost of confidence—you know what works for me every time?"

"What?" she asks, exiting the stall and washing her hands.

"I think you need some pumps—what is your shoe size?"

JON

Hearing Tae cry over her weight broke my heart into a million pieces. I knew she was struggling with the trust fund girls at her private school, but now knowing her fucking mother was chipping away at her self-image made me so mad.

The attorney I saw just a couple of weeks ago—funnily enough, the first day I met DJ—was already preparing another appeal to my visitation rights agreement with Miranda, especially now that she is living in Florida. I wish I had grounds to ask for custody, but as Ramsay is funding her shark lawyers, it is difficult winning a custody case against a birth mother who is married to a billionaire. But with my sister getting older, I am hoping she would also enjoy seeing me more, and can tell that to a judge.

One thing that lifted my spirits was seeing DJ help Tae. She dropped me the second she caught a girl crying, then made sure she was OK and offered to hurt whoever upset her. Sitting outside the restrooms, I felt a tug deep inside me, knowing she was not only bold and smart but too kind and would fight for those in need. I also felt like a king when she talked about the 'hottest man' she ever saw kissing her silly.

I couldn't stop myself from touching her when she was again so close to me, and when she bit my neck, my cock sprung to life in an instant. Tracing where she left a little tooth mark on my skin, I smile tugs at my lips, but I do not know what to do with her. I want her, but with her working for me, there was no way around it. HR would have my head. The gossip will put a real dent in any relationship between us. I can't fire her, and I can't fuck her. I was stuck.

The door to the toilets opens and DJ is first out, but this time about four inches shorter, as she is now sporting a pair of flats. Behind her, my sister struts up with a sly smile on her, as she walks out with her head held high, wearing some familiar strappy sandals.

"Ladies, looking good." I nod in acknowledgment. "Ready to go back to the party?"

They exchange a couple of confident glances and then both of them square their shoulders.

"Oh, beyond ready. Especially ready to take someone on right about now," Dahlia announces.

"Easy there, million-dollar-baby. Let's not forget we have press here. I do agree we need to find Miranda and have a few words with her. Tae, would you like to go out on the terrace? I think they have some presentations on the volunteering activities available."

My sister is looking at me like I am trying to play her, which I was, forgetting she isn't five anymore.

"Fine, *Jon*. I'll go check out the projects, but only because I genuinely enjoy volunteering. But please don't fight with my mom. I don't want to get in trouble. Pleeease," she pleads, making big eyes at me.

"OK, I won't make a scene. Off you go, kid."

"Don't call me kid!" she counters, but heads to the exit, slightly unsure of herself on the heels but getting a bit of swagger in her step.

"Thank you again. For the shoes as well," I tell DJ, who was looking at my exchange with Tae, smiling her cute little smirk.

"Nothing to it. Even warrior princesses need their armor." She gently elbows me, but before continuing, she stops and stares, seething at something in the background. "Well, well, Richard is here, as predicted. And he is with Miranda. So, caveman, are you ready for that 'talk'?"

As I turn towards the pair, I confirm, "I am right behind you, as I technically promised not to cause a scene—but I didn't hear you promise anything—you got dibs." From the very real smile on her face, I know I hit the bullseye. I reckon I dug myself out at least halfway from the hole I got in with DJ after last Saturday's dumb dash I did.

With me looming behind her with what I hope is a murderous glare, my little spitfire and I make our way to our rivals for a long overdue chat.

DJ

Walking towards my ex again after not seeing him for about six months was surprisingly anticlimactic. I had no feelings about him at all anymore, just perhaps slight queasiness at noticing his smug face as he was blabbering away with some business people with Naomi Campbell's evil lookalike next to him. Richard Simmons, the fucking snake!

I do, however, have a feeling of safe-ness knowing Jon watches my back, as a great defender ready to help, but letting me lead. I am woman enough to admit the moment he said I got dibs it made me all giddy. Combined with seeing him with his sister earlier had all my mushy feelings flare up, making me even more resolute in my decision to clear the air with him. Even though I am still a bit apprehensive about starting something with someone I worked with again, there is this bond between us I needed to accept.

I stop straight between my ex-husband and his audience. Jon's presence makes the crowd scatter, with only the four of us facing off.

"Richard, I heard you were in town… how is that software going? Easy build-up, is it? Ready to launch?" I stomp on the pressure point. Easy, my ass. Without my knowledge, he would scramble to even know where to begin.

I can see him almost frothing at the mouth, his dark eyes enraged, his arms crossed.

"It's going great," he says punctuating 'great' as if I would ever believe a word he said. "I understand you now work for him." He nods his head at the man behind me, but instead of stopping there, he continues being himself, "I hear he sticks his dick in everything with a skirt, so you may want to watch yourself."

I can feel Jon getting ready to advance, and sense him clenching his fists, but I shake my head slightly. My ex-husband needs to find some better comebacks if he thinks some sex shaming would trigger me.

"That's cute and not at all childish, but I can take care of myself. And I see you are working… Oh, that was it, you are working! Good for you!"

Before Richard makes a bigger fool of himself, the woman next to him barges in, her sweet, sickly tone grating my eardrums.

"Ah Richard, you didn't say your ex-wife enjoys heckling people. Perhaps she needs to get back behind her computer and pretend to code some more. Or maybe she shouldn't, but then ICE will send you back to the third world country you came from. You and your leeching family, fresh off a Cuban boat."

I am taken aback by her commentary and even though I was supposed to not react, I growl at her.

"You did not just insult my family, you bitch." Immediately, my patience evaporates. I almost launch myself at her, only to be caught by a large warm arm around my middle, holding me in place.

"Hey there, Cobra Kai, it's what she wants you to lose your temper and strike first. Look around us, DJ, the press is watching," Jon speaks next to my ear. "Miranda, I see you haven't learned any manners, still a conniving witch who can only insult people who are better than you."

Before the Lexington shrew can answer, it's my former spouse who is continuing the show.

"What the fuck!" he yells. "He calls you DJ? Are you serious now?" He moves towards Jon, who tries to pull me behind him again, but I don't let him. I can—and will enjoy— kneeing my ex in the balls if I must.

"What's your problem, Rich? You think you own half my name also? Stealing half my money and trying to slander me was not enough?"

"It's not my fault you got caught with the police car on your doorstep. You threatened me! I had to tell the people at Hove who they had in their team! Also, I most certainly helped you code 'Zephyr'!"

"How about you shut up before you cause a bigger scene, Simmons?" the man next to me intervenes. "I suspect DJ and myself have quite a lot of dirty laundry we could air out, if you both want. But I recommend you settle the fuck down and let the grown-ups speak," Jon curtly snarls, looking at both of our enemies.

I can see something sinister flashing on Miranda's face like she just caught onto something, and she can't wait to use it. She takes a sip out of her champagne glass as she smiles disturbingly, matching a Bond villain, minus the white cat.

Jon either misses her smirk or wants to prove his point. Approaching the subject we originally came here for, slightly glazing over the 'not making a scene' agreement, but I can't say I blame him, he goes for it.

"I overheard what you told Tae off about her eating dessert. I also saw her running in the bathroom crying—is that how you treat your daughter? There is nothing wrong with her weight, you harpy."

"Ah, my dear former stepson, you have NO business telling me how to raise my daughter. However, I see you found yourself a little Latina toy to defend from the big bad wolves. You always liked them lively. But is she aware of all the parties? Or…" she lowers her voice and approaches me directly, "the drugs?"

I don't have to turn to him to know Jon is either frozen or steaming mad, and I only take a moment to tilt my head at her. This hoe thinks I can be fooled that easily, especially after they clearly sent those fake news to the Observer.

"Oh, dear Mir Mir," I start in a condescending tone, "someone can't get to the grapes I see. Unsure if green is really your color." I grin and move in front of Jon again. With a lick of my lips, I continue, "Do not worry your pretty head Mir, I know… a lot… about him." Her grinding teeth tell me I hit my mark. She is going to run through her veneers at this rate.

"Fuck—you really are sleeping with him?" Richard stutters, waking up from the word hiatus he was in.

"Sleeping?" I add in a slightly serial killer-y tone, "Not sleeping as much. I just... like rewiring his flaps."

Several things happen at once, as though we are in a slapstick comedy. My ex's face reddens close to the shade of a ripe tomato. Miranda chokes on her champagne and it partially comes out of her nose. Jon pulls me out of the way, so Julia Li gets a 'spit and bubbly' special on her golden dress and squeaks loudly. All the while, several camera flashes go off.

I want to get us out of there, but Jon still has something to end the discussion with.

"Just so you know, Miranda, I hope your lawyers are ready, as I am coming for Tae. She deserves better than you. Come on DJ, let's go. We have things to do." He takes me by the elbow and drags me away, leaving our two competitors gaping at us. Cameras flash again, and I hope they got some great shots.

Jon

I get us out of the restaurant before strangling Miranda or punching Richard, so I call that a PR win. DJ is quiet, covering her mouth with her hand. That is, until we go outside, and I see what she is really covering is a burst of giggles. She starts laughing while hiding her face in my chest. I pull her with me, moving us down the boardwalk, far away from the prying eyes of Julia's guests.

Reaching a bench, I sit down, but she remains up between my thighs and puts her hands on my shoulders.

"So that was quite fun, eh? Minus the parts where you were called a 'manwhore' and I was pretty much called 'the help'."

"That could have gone better probably, but I am glad I told her about my intentions with Tae. And your ex-husband is really a piece of work. There must have been a lot of tequila in Vegas that you ended up marrying him!"

She snorts a "No comment!"

A slight breeze from the ocean brings her scent to life, and her hair moves in the wind. She is so close to me and her boobs are exactly at my eye level. The blood goes straight to my dick again, watching this vision in yellow touch me. I put my hands on her hips, trying to push her away, but she resists.

"Jon, I have been wanting to ask you something. Do you like me?"

"Umm," I babble, shocked at her directness, not quite finding coherent words. "It doesn't matter. You work for me." I pull my palms off her and put them on my knees.

Her radiant smile is brighter than the sun. She is undeterred and puts my hands back on her and then takes my face in her palms. I feel her delicate skin through the crop areas of her dress and can't stop myself from caressing her gently.

"How about you answer the question, caveman? Come on, be honest. Do you want to kiss me again?"

"More than anything," comes out of my mouth before stopping myself as I look up into her beautiful eyes.

"That is the right answer." She lowers her lips to mine but stops before pressing them on and taking me out of my misery. Her sexy voice is soft as she tenderly caresses my beard and I pull her closer to me. "The reason that is the correct answer is that... Jon, I do not actually work for you. You are not my boss."

"What? What do you mean?" I panic. "Your contract..." Shit, I really should not leave all contracts supervision to Mike!"

Without moving, she explains exactly what a moron I am.

"You big idiot, I have my own company—you didn't hire me directly. We have a collaboration contract between our two companies. I do not report to you. It is true we work together—which is not ideal—but there are no reporting lines between us. Caveman…"

The neurons in my brain fire madly. I look at her face and she is smiling even more than before.

"Fuck—I really am an idiot!" I exclaim and finally, I grip her hair and do what I never should have stopped doing last time—pull her lips on mine.

This is not slow like in the car or hurried like in the shop. It is much the same as raising the cup at the end of the race, intense and euphoric. Her tongue sweeps against mine, and my other hand grabs her ass as she moans in my mouth. My hard cock pressed against her leg. She rakes her fingers in my hair just as she fancies, making me groan.

When I pause the kiss again, it isn't at all the same as last weekend, but more in line with what I described to her I would do.

"Don't you dare stop!" she seethes at me, but I just flash her a smile.

"Don't worry Avril, you are only getting what you were warned about!"

Before any more protests or idiocy and time-wasting from my part, I look around for any pesky reporters and I lift her over my shoulder. Shamelessly, I hold a palm over her ass keeping her dress in place—perhaps coping another feel—and run towards my car over the sounds of a squeaking DJ.

DJ

Jon probably broke about ten speed limits in the brief five minutes' drive to his townhouse. All the while keeping his right hand on my thigh, gently caressing, never moving higher than the hem on my skirt, sometimes making little circles or just touching me under the seam of my dress and driving me absolutely insane.

My thong was soaked by the time he stopped in his garage, and I was hot all over, looking forward to whatever my caveman had in store for me. I have been carried before but never experienced the possession I felt from his searing hand on my ass as he hurried to his SUV.

My door gets yanked open before I manage to take in any of the other cars in the garage or anything around me, hearing exactly what every full-blooded woman needs, as Jon pulls me out of his car and says kissing and nipping my neck.

"I have been wanting to taste you ever since I saw you. Spread you on every surface in my house and lap you up until you drench my face with your cream."

Fuck. Me. That was something else!

But I was not a sweet, naïve girl without my own tricks.

I lower one of my hands around his built torso, gently caressing his groin over his trousers, while murmuring in his ear and scratching his chin with my nails.

"How about... you eat me up on the hood of your Range Rover? You know, as repayment for last Saturday's blue lady balls you left me with," I state and squeeze his hard cock.

He groans and his "Fuck me!" is far more vocal than mine. As he takes his jacket off in no time, lays it on top of his warm car then picks me up and within seconds, I stop thinking and lift my legs, put my heels on the bonnet and slowly, oh so slowly, staring straight at him, I part my knees and pull my dress up.

He watches me like a hunter in the savannah, blistering heat in his eyes, hands on the side of my ankles. His nostrils flare as he spots my yellow thong against my brown skin, the wetness probably visible.

I raise the stakes by starting to run a hand on my inner thigh, pushing my skirt up around my waist with the other and spreading my legs even more. As my fingers touch my underwear, he snaps and pounces on me.

But instead of going for my core, he hustles his tongue into my mouth again, dragging me closer to the edge of the car, and pulling my hair. His fingers descend on my back, and I hear my zipper opening, my arms being removed from the top of my dress and in no time, my garment is hunched around my middle.

"I need repayment for not seeing these tits last week," is what Jon says as he pushes the straps of my bra down and lowers the yellow satin cups and with an ear-splitting 'Jesus!', then puts his mouth on one of my breasts. His tongue swivels around my hard nipple, and as I whimper loudly, I pick up a sexy rumble of male pride from him. When his hand finds my other nipple and pinches it, my back arches like a goddamn porn star.

He doesn't stop but moves to suck and tease my other bud, and all I can do is keep him in place grasping his hair, his scent enveloping me. My moans must be ridiculous, but Jon is not only undeterred, but seems more and more spurred on with each of my wails.

Suddenly, he lowers my back on the SUV, and his fingers curl around the sides of my panties as he gently pulls them down my legs, and then I can see them flying down the halfway through his garage. The hunter is back, laser-focused on my center as he reopens my thighs himself.

"Hell, DJ, look at that pink pussy, so beautiful," he praises as he runs his knuckle up and down my slit, barely touching me. "So pink and beautiful, bare and wet for me, just waiting for me to run my tongue all over it."

"Oh my God, Jon, stop talking to it and lick it!"

"Shh my impatient and tumultuous skater girl. I want to savor his moment, the seconds before I taste you for the first time, before our world explodes," he continues his torment, using the least amount of physical contact, the tip of his finger grazing my labia. His left hand replicates

116

the movement on the peak of my nipple, the same strenuous, barely there touch, duplicating my distress.

My head rolls under these ministrations, and I try to grab for something to hold on but there is nothing but the shiny metallic warm car around me, so I settle to clutch the edge of Jon's jacket under me as I drown in the unexpecting pleasure from the dual caress.

With my eyes closed, I only feel the wetness of his tongue over my pussy, and I cry out loud. He starts licking me in earnest, in circles similar to the ones he made with his palm on my leg earlier, then his lips suck on my mound, and I begin to shiver, my climax within reach already.

He knows how close I am as he adds a finger in my opening, curling it slightly and stroking, and still nibbling and teasing my sensitive folds. I feel a graze of his teeth on my clit which travels up my spine, increasing my moans and his manly sexy growls. His tongue swipes and swirls between my legs, savaging me.

It isn't the second finger in my canal which unravels me, but the desire I see in him as I open my eyes, screaming his name as I come watching him feasting on me.

My lower limbs fall against the bumper as I pant through the aftershocks of my amazing orgasm. Jon's face is sporting a well-pleased grin, as he moves himself up my body, his hands worshipping my sides, then my breasts, and then lifting me up so I can taste myself on his lips.

The kiss starts slowly but ignites as I lock my ankles behind him and drag myself to put my arms around his neck. As I grind my centre on his groin, my throbbing pussy is wetting his slacks as our tongues tangle. He is hard as steel, and I know he will not last long if I keep rubbing myself on him, but what I am feeling is too amazing to stop.

"Bed!" is all he says as he picks me up off the hood and, still ravaging my mouth, starts taking me into the main house. His grip on my bottom never falters as he takes me up a flight of stairs and into what I suppose is his bedroom, though I can't see much of my surroundings as I am blinded by the magnificent man holding me, kneading my ass cheeks and responding to my kisses with fervor.

I get thrown on his massive bed and I scramble to take my dress off as it was still hanging around my waist. I freeze when I look at Jon's naked chest and incredible tattoos again, still marveling at the man's delectable form.

"Ogling me, Avril?" he asks, but he was doing the same thing, so I play into it, spreading my arms on his bed, stretching like a cat. I hear his belt buckle open as he removes his trousers and boxers, and then he hisses, fisting his thick dick, observing me. We are both fully naked now, me spread on this dark gray comforter, him looming over me, rubbing himself, watching me transfixed.

"Come here caveman," comes out more as a gasp, filled with want, opening my legs again, showing him where he needs to be.

He reaches into one of his wooden nightstands, picks up a condom and starts rolling it on, our eyes never leaving each other.

I yelp as he grabs my ankles and drags me to him. Jon stares at my cunt like at art as he begins sliding the head of his massive shaft up and down my folds, continuing the maddening teasing he seems to enjoy torturing me with.

"I wanted to make this last—to hear you wanting me and begging me to fuck you, to plug you up with my cock, but looking at you here, at my mercy in my bed makes me just do this." He thrusts in, filling me to the hilt.

I cry in pleasure at the fullness, bowing my back in rapture. Putting my calves on his shoulders, Jon starts to move, possessed, holding my legs up, the angle making him touch deep inside me. My tits bounce as he snaps his hips again and again.

"Jon oh my god!" I scream as he fucks me hard and fast, then lowers one of my legs and pushes against the other, changing the orientation, and plunging in me even more. I am lightheaded and feverish all over. All I sense is him moving inside me, his eyes on me lustful.

Over and over, his strokes possess me. He buries himself in my sheath repeatedly, as all I can do is enjoy the ride, shivering and moaning.

I explode when he moves his hand over my breast and pinches my nipple so hard I might bruise, but the touch of pain pushes me over the edge, yelling again.

My orgasm unleashes something in him, his movements erratic and overpowering, and when I feel him shuddering, throbbing inside me, he throws his head back and roars as he empties himself. He is magnificent as he comes, my caveman, appearing carved by Rodin himself—I want to see him like this again and again.

He rests in the same position for a moment, both of us catching our breath, then gently bites the inside of my calf and goes to get rid of the condom and clean up, leaving me reeling, simply staring at the ceiling in awe of what just happened.

I don't wait long as he climbs on top of me, crushing his mouth on me as I drag my nails over his back and rub my shin against his leg.

"Hi Avril," he says as he boxes me in with his muscular forearms.

"Hi to you too, caveman." I smile and run my fingers through his hair, tenderly massaging his head, winning me a rumble of pleasure from him. He leans and peppers my shoulder and neck with kisses as he moves slightly off me and begins caressing me.

"You are so beautiful," Jon starts. "This neck." He kisses it. "This collarbone." He runs his finger gently over it. "And these tits. Fuck—these tits I can't believe I waited so long to taste these!" He takes a tip in his mouth and sucks on it as I heave. "To touch them." He uses his palm to fondle my other breast, still keeping suction on my nipple. My nub is so hard as his tongue twirls around it, and just when I can't take it anymore, he moves to the other and all I can think of is to get him inside me, ideally while he still tends to my boobs.

But it is my turn to play, so I get my vagina in check, to push him on his back and start tracing his chest with my finger, my hair falling on his shoulder.

"You are the one to talk, hot man, these muscles," I add while kiss his peck, "these abs." I run my palm on his flat stomach and following his happy-trail I reach his thickening penis. "And this cock of yours," I caress it gently along its already hardening length and Jon's breath catches. "I think I am well within my repayment rights to have a serious conversation with this big dick." His eyes turn sparkling as I lower myself in the bed, mapping his front with my nails, enjoying the hissing sounds he makes.

Placing my lips a hairbreadth from his member, I whisper staring straight at his face, "Because you somehow believed I don't need 30 people working for me to create the weather predictor, that I could do it all by myself... well, you deserve a treat."

"Treat?" he gasps. "I am surely treated right now just by having you hovering over my cock."

"Oh, the charmer came out to play?" I smile, not awaiting his answer, but flatten my tongue and run it over his shaft from base to tip, doing a little swirl around the head, licking a bead of fluid which causes Jon to growl. I continue taking just the top in my mouth, keeping eye contact, but hold his balls in my hand and start massaging them.

He jerks and moans, "Fuck... me!"

Picking a page out of Jon's book, I slowly, incredibly slowly start taking him fully in, and when he hits the back of my throat, I relax and welcome him further in. Jon's eyes close, this incredible man completely surrendering to me. I commence sucking in earnest, using one hand at his base, rubbing him and the other on his balls, bobbing my head, marveling at him lost in pleasure.

He doesn't thrust in the beginning, leaving me in charge until I hollow my cheeks and the suction makes him move his hips, starting to fuck my mouth. He makes a fist with my hair as he moves deep down my throat, and I moan over his powerful pushes.

"I can feel that through my balls. Fuck! You take me so well."

I can't speak so full of him but continue playing with his testicles, using my nails to press gently behind them, in the magic zone which makes him move faster and faster. The noises coming out of him increase, words turn to gibberish and then he freezes, and I feel his release down my throat; I assist by drinking him down, licking every drop, while still touching the place behind his balls, extending his orgasm.

He flumps back, drained, and I move up and rest my head on his shoulder. His arm pulls me to him, and I put a leg over his.

"Fucking hell woman, that was quite a treat!" He notes in the end.

I chuckle, burying my face in his chest. "You are not so bad yourself, mister."

He draws little circles on my hip with his hand and I hold him tighter, putting my arm around his waist, both of us enjoying the silence and contentment between us.

"Seriously, Jon, did you not read the contract at all?" I lift my head and look over at him.

"Honestly, I didn't even think about it—Mike usually takes care of that, I have a zillion suppliers, engineering etc. on my roster... I do not know why I assumed I was interviewing you, sounds like you were interviewing ME!"

I laugh at that and kiss his cheek. "Now you are getting it, caveman. You paid for exclusive usage, but my company isn't a subcontractor to yours, more like a partner. I get access to your planes for testing, you use my software. As to why I was at your office for the meeting... I just didn't prioritize renting an official headquarters yet. I know, CEO of the year, I am not. But with the move and all my staff preferring working from home, that was not high on my 'to do' list. Some really good people work for me, with years of experience. They don't need a lot of supervision, so I can code as well. It helps I have a couple of great project managers as well, who supervise day-to-day activities." I explain how I can be both a manager and work on writing software. I plaster myself over him more, the heat coming from his body as addictive as his cologne.

"When Richard started badmouthing me at Hove, and my boss said it would be best if we don't disrupt the workplace with our personal issues instead of taking my side knowing damn well my ex had no part in my code, I decided that going at it alone was the way forward. My team there agreed to leave with me. Since then, I have picked up a few others. It's not thousands like you have at McAv, but it's enough for now." I shrug.

"I suppose that's why you were reluctant to start anything with me? After the Hove mess?"

I nod in agreement, but he continues on a different path.

"Wow! That is pretty brave to give them the middle finger. I did not want to be CEO. I never thought it was for me. If my father wouldn't have dropped the company on me, I would have never come back."

"Shove it down your throat, did he?" I poke at his side.

"More like guilt tripped me. He said I either came back home and took over or he would give it to Miranda. I agreed, but never knew he was ill. When his lawyer called, I was on the slopes of Tignes. Scared out of my mind, a 23-year-old with no experience of running anything besides a bar tab. So yeah, brave taking the risk yourself."

"Well, from where I am sitting, you seem to be doing pretty good. The company is in the black, your employees have yet to push you in front of a moving propeller, and from what I saw today, the town folk also think you are doing a great job. Also, I am surprised he didn't groom you from infancy to take over."

"Ha, those vultures at the luncheon! It's just schmoozing, really. And no, he did not tell me stories of mergers and acquisitions while bouncing me on his knee. My mom and I weren't so much of a priority for him, so the company was more of an abstract for me growing up. I did spend my summers in the hangar fixing planes with the techs, and that I truly enjoyed, but my father wasn't the man to pick up a screwdriver. When my mother moved to the South of France, I decided that jet skiing in the summer and snowboarding in the winter were the way to go. I have to admit I got in some pretty crazy situations; some I am not that proud of." Jon exhales slowly and stares at the ceiling.

"Haven't we all? Suspect the drugs Miranda was trying to point at earlier were part of that?"

"Yeah, I was young and dumb, and ran with the wrong crowd, tried a few things, but it's been at least... I don't know... fourteen. Fifteen? years since I took anything, so she is grasping at straws. My dad's death and Tae's birth changed matters for me."

"Hey, I was young also and some of the stupid stuff I did—let's never go there, though my sister will probably tell you a few very embarrassing stories. So how did you manage with McAv just given to you?" I gently caress his arms, tracing the designs of his tattoos.

"Luckily, I do have a Business major so that helped a bit when I got handed over the proverbial golden key to the kingdom. Though, randomly it seems what you appreciate most is my English lit minor, you little mischief maker."

"That explains a lot, actually." I giggle, remembering his preference for 'big' words.

"It was Mike who really came through. She knew all about the contracts and I left them to her, as I took on more technical and supplier relations. Been working fine, I think. Well, it did, until someone threw a spanner in the works, and I got a very disruptive non-employee, one I can't seem to get out of my mind. She tastes so good, too."

All of a sudden, I am on my back and Jon accidentally discovers one of my best-kept secrets in the world as he nibbles on my side.

"Oh—what do we have here—is the fearless ball-buster Dahlia Jara... ticklish?" he asks in delight as I squirm and squeal as he keeps nipping, holding me down. "Well, well, I seem to have found your Achilles heel."

"Oh yeah, you would be wrong!" I manage to say as I try to roll away, but I fake-fail miserably.

"I need to investigate this matter more, in great detail" he flashes his dimple at me—the one which I won't admit to being one of my weaknesses either—and proceeds to tickle me more, until I slap his ass telling him to stop it.

"Ah, there is one thing I wanted to ask as well." Jon stops entertaining himself. "What was with the outfit?"

"Which one?" I pretend not to recognize what he means.

"Come on, Avril, you know I am not asking about the heart-attack-generating dresses. Out with it or I am sure I can find how you can resist some... torture." He grins at me and licks his lips.

Though that sounds quite interesting, and I take a note to order a feather, I suppose I need to come clean.

"Lost a bet. Actually, I lost a poker hand."

"Vegas again?"

"Worse... my mother's kitchen table. To a 10-year-old. A 10-year-old I am convinced counts cards, but little fucker won't fess up."

Jon snickers against my stomach, tickling me with his beard this time, as I continue describing another less-than-proud moment.

"My nephew Javi—my sister Laura's son—is going through a card phase. Taught himself how to play poker from YouTube. Somehow he convinced me to play with him. Naively, I believed we would be gambling for candy. But no, the kid goes for the jugular. We start on candy as I thought, but within 5 hands I am wiped clean. He sports a knowing look at me and says, 'let's play for some real stakes, auntie DJ—dares or favors'."

"Jeez, that sounds like you should have stopped right there before getting hustled."

"I really, reaaaally, should have. By the end of the evening, I was down two trips to Disney, one ice cream for dinner weekend, and then, the after worse hand in the history of card games... he demanded a trip to Atlantic City which I wouldn't budge on. My sister would have killed me and he couldn't have gotten into the casinos either—though apparently he wanted to watch the casino floor from the balcony or something like that. So, Javier went for his fallback plan—as every kid obviously has one—the Dare."

"And his dare was... shorts?"

"Not shorts, you dolt!" I mock punch him again. "I was dared to dress like I did in high school for an entire week. He saw the pictures and thought I was cool—which I evidently am. I am quite lucky it wasn't the week with the interview. That would have been something about me rolling in my 20-year-old sneakers on my board—which I am literally the worst on. I would have probably run someone over."

"The coolest aunt indeed," Jon laughs his full-on laugh again, "so skateboarding is not your strong suit?"

"Hell no, I only tried it to get boys!" That makes him tickle me again, mumbling, "I'll show you a boy in a minute!"

He only goes on for a bit until he is sufficiently amused by my giggles and continues the conversation, "You should have him meet Nathan. His actual business is making playing cards; at least you'll know he didn't doctor the cards next time. My mate is an excellent poker player himself. Won a bunch of championships in college."

"Nathan, your flirty friend? Yeah—my sister would really like me to introduce her son to the card-shark Don Juan

127

of Florida so he can pick up some more bad habits." I roll my eyes at the idea, but perhaps it has some merit.

"Har, har. He isn't that bad actually, more posturing than anything—shit! Forgot to text Tae to see if she's alright." He is up in an instant, shuffling through his clothes to find his phone, causing me to pause to admire that firm ass of his, biting my lower lip and thinking of biting something else.

"Ogling again?" he asks without turning, knowing exactly why I am so quiet.

"More like objectifying, actually," I confess shamelessly. He shakes his head at me, then plops back on the sheets, texting with his right hand, but with his left holding my boob.

"What? I am doing some objectifying of my own, maybe a bit of fondling the CEO in my bed," he answers without looking at me when I give him a silent glare.

He finishes his texts, then puts down his phone and does a bit more than just fondling.

JON

I woke up first after our post-fondling nap, and left DJ sleeping like a starfish in my bed, putting on some shorts and a t-shirt. It is surprising how much space she occupies but can't seem to mind at all—even the occasional forearm to my face was quite endearing.

The sun is about to set over Kerrington, and I stop on the kitchen balcony to admire the sunset. My phone buzzes and it's Nate, and I had forgotten he was back in town this weekend again.

"Hey Jon, what's up? Want to go for a drink tonight? Maybe pick up a chick or two this time? You never said what you did last Saturday when you abandoned me at the bar."

"Nah, already have company. Go on without me. I didn't leave you like an unwanted puppy—you had your own ride and I doubt you left by yourself."

"You got a girl over? Anyone I know? Perhaps a certain hot brunette?" I can hear him grinning through the phone.

"No comment and how about you fuck right off?"

"Oh! It is her! Ha-ha! I knew she was more than an employee!"

"Yeah, turns out she wasn't even my employee—I created this story in my head that she works for me, when she actually has her own company and is just collaborating with us."

"Hilarious! What a dumbass you are!" he correctly names it. "At least you cleared the air... so this one has enough personality, I hope."

"More than plenty. She's pretty awesome." I look longingly toward the house. "By the way, I ran into Tae today—she looked great. I am partially glad the bitch moved back to Florida if I get to spend more time with my sister now."

"That is good news—when you see her, let me know. I would love to visit my favorite 'almost niece'. So, I suspect you also saw her mother? Has Beelzebub's relative graced our fine county with her 'Presence'?" I hear my friend cringing over the phone. He was there with me when my father first brought Miranda over, with her 'you bow to me' attitude and ridiculous expectations.

Luckily, I was not a kid, and I easily told her off, much to her chagrin.

"Unfortunately, I have also seen the witch. Still the same vitriol out of her. I almost lost it today, I swear! She upset Tabitha, then insulted DJ, whom I had to stop from throttling Miranda, but if the reporters weren't there, I wouldn't have."

"Sounds like she got even worse since going to New York. At least she didn't come onto you again?"

"I would say no, but interestingly, Dahlia figured out the shrew did not like me being there with her. I think she was trying to goad us into getting into a fight with them so they can show us as unhinged in the media." I conclude, between the idiotic dialogue earlier and the reporter last week.

"Man, you have your work cut out for you—let me know if I can help with anything—but at least your giiirl-frieeend was there for you," he snickers again.

"Dude, we are almost in our forties. You are allowed not to sound like you are still in high school!" I make fun of my best friend but looking at the time I must go take care of my brunette. "Right man, got to order some food. Catch you later!"

"Later Romeo, be good." He finishes with exaggerated kissing sounds, which cause me to shake my head. I may be a dumbass, but Nathan is a childish dumbass.

I open an app and order us some pizzas and get a couple of beers from the fridge, but before going back upstairs, I am awed by a goddess sitting on my sofa.

She is wearing the pinstripe shirt I had on earlier and, from what I can see—only my shirt. I suspect her under-wear is somewhere in the garage. I grin faced with such hardship and cross my arms, leaning against the entrance and admiring her some more from the side of the room.

Hair again piled erratically on her head, mouth in a tight line and eyes focusing on the TV screen, as she drives as Luigi in a Mario kart race on my console. She is absolutely adorable, huffing and puffing, trying to overtake Bowser, moving her whole body with the track. She is almost at the last turn, so she accelerates and gets the first position just before the checkered line and gives a little whoop of joy, which makes me want to throw that controller and kiss her.

I put the beers on the walnut table and do just that, ignoring her weak complaints, picking her up easily and putting her across in my lap, my mouth on hers, hungry to taste her. I can't seem to have enough of holding her little body and touching her. Feeling her tongue against mine and hearing one of her moans vibrating against my chest.

"I guess my fantasy of having a half-naked woman playing on my console can now be ticked off my bucket list," I add, hugging DJ tighter.

"That is me, fulfilling your deepest wishes," she quips and puts her arms around my shoulders, and I suspect she doesn't realize how close she is to the truth. "Is there any food here or are you a 'strictly beer in the fridge' kind of guy?"

"Oh, there is some food—though I confess I get meals delivered. Beer, we are stocked, don't worry, I hand her a bottle. But I ordered some pizzas."

"Pizza!" She beams as if I helicoptered in a chef from Miami. "One of my favorite five-a-day. Good thing you have foodstuff, as you probably don't want me burning your kitchen down. But I think there is a serious discussion we need to have, which is quite critical to whether you get laid again." Her severe tone may cause me some concern if it wasn't for the sneaky look on her and playful smile. "Let's see you... choose your player..." She pulls the second controller from behind a throw pillow, warning me, "You better not touch Luigi! He is mine!" The cutest, most non-threatening Luigi-protective growl makes me laugh, and I put her back on the sofa with a peck on the side of her head.

I pick Princess Peach, which is obviously the right choice, as for the next hour or so I get rewarded with several mind-numbing kisses as we play our game and polish our pizza.

"At least we didn't have to wait for dial-up to fire up before we played," she reminisces from the old days of the internet.

"Yeah, when we blocked the phone line for hours on end." I smile, also recalling the trials of getting online twenty years ago.

DJ, however, suddenly puts down the controller and looks at me with delight, a blinding grin on her face.

"Phone lines! 90s! Shit! I know why you have such a high phone bill at McAv" she hoots with an 'a-ha, the butler did it!' face.

"Huh? We have a dial-up at the office?"

"No, silly—but that would have also been a clever idea. Come on, let's go!" She gets up and runs upstairs.

"What? Where are you going?" I follow her two stairs at a time, and I see her naked and pulling her dress over her head. My other head has some better ideas, but I realize there's no stopping her.

"WE are going to McAv," she mentions as she puts Tae's flats on. "I just had a lightbulb moment, but I need to see it with my own eyes."

"OK, Avril, to the office we go," I give in, as it's clearly the easiest way to find out what is happening. "Let me get some shoes on and my phone and wallet." I say, but not before slapping her ass. She gives me the evil eye, but I think she enjoys that.

The garage is a bit of a mess. My suit jacket is spread on the hood of my SUV, reminding me with pride of having DJ's juices all over my face, her bra is on the floor, car door still half open. Her thong is nowhere in sight, which means that she has no underwear under her flowy dress, causing my cock to stir.

"Don't even think about it, you horny caveman!" she cautions, as clearly my dimple is making it hard to hide where my mind just went. "We can re-enact the scene later, but for now we have bigger fish to fry." DJ picks up her bra, puts it in her bag, and looks around for her panties but shrugs as she can't see them either and gets in the car.

Having no alternative to following my woman's orders, I put the jacket on the back of a chair and start driving us to my office, not at all thinking of her bare pussy within reach.

JON

The floors are deserted on a Saturday night, just as I expected. My weekend security guards look at us funny, but they can't say 'no' to the CEO strutting in whenever he feels like, even though their boss is dressed for the gym and is joined by a woman in a yellow cocktail dress and freshly fucked hair.

DJ spares no time in going to the top floor, then making her way down, getting under every desk, opening every door, and looking at every printer. I can only follow, trying to make sense of what she is looking for and enjoying the view of her bottom whenever she bends over. There must be some rewards after all for dragging me on her scavenger hunt.

"May I ask you something, Jon?" She looks at me after failing to find whatever she is digging for in one of the maintenance cupboards.

"Go on..."

"It's actually why you reacted so 'caveman'-like in the hangar when I asked what's the history with Miranda."

"Oh—frankly, I was a bit surprised you were that interested, and a bit apprehensive about washing our family's laundry to a semi-stranger. You have to understand when she met my dad, I was abroad and didn't think too much of my dad's 'flavor of the month'. Then she got a ring on her finger and started acting like an entitled bitch. She went from remodeling the whole house to demanding holidays and gifts from my dad. The worst was her trying to act like she was my actual mother, giving me directions and trying to forbid me from going out."

"I suppose that went well," she comments as she crawls under a table.

"As well as can be expected. I told her to fuck off as I was not a minor and that she should mind her own business. Things got a bit uncomfortable when she changed gears, and started wearing revealing bikinis around the house, accidentally dropping her towel around me after a shower and being suggestive, though not overly open, that she wanted me for other purposes." The cringing look on her face matches my own.

"Nathan was her first target—he was more shell-shocked than anything and literally ran out on her when she came into the kitchen wearing nothing but lingerie. She must have found out afterward that his family disowned his father, so his O'Malley surname would not bring her fame and fortune, and tried to sink her claws in me—I think she knew my father was not well and imagined herself switching McMasters."

"That is a tad disgusting. Why would you ever want your dad's leftovers?"

"No idea, but that's how her mind works, or maybe she did that before. In any case, she got nowhere with me, and probably this is part of why she hates my guts—the one that got away and all that!"

"But I think her not getting the company is also a part of that?" DJ rightly guesses again.

"Exactly! But I told you my dad had the vision of our name being carried on, so he never wanted Miranda to get any shares or the like. If she wouldn't have pulled a positive pregnancy test and—at my insistence—took a DNA test, she wouldn't even have gotten the millions in the will, which were really for Tae."

"That explains quite a lot. Thank you for telling me." She gives me a quick kiss but before getting us both worked up again, she frowns, looking around us, her attention going back to the search. "I don't understand where it can be," she mumbles in frustration, but turns to me again as clearly, she has more questions.

"Jon, is your sister really OK with Miranda? Didn't really think her comment about the cake was at all appropriate."

"I thought so until now," I sigh. "I knew Miranda was not actually involved much in her upbringing. Tae had a really great nanny growing up who basically raised her, but she retired a few months back, as to be fair she was getting a bit too old to be babysat. I know she's usually left alone, and I try to get as involved as I can, but it was hard when they were living in New York."

"Well, at least you can get to see her more now that they are in Florida," she echoes my previous statement and I nod.

Dahlia frowns more and more as we approach the basement, not having found whatever she was trying to locate. We get to the IT department and realize I haven't been there in a while, ever since we had a proper IT team on site, not just offshore tech support and a weekly equipment van coming to give people new laptops and all that. Despite the brooding ambiance, it looks akin to a gamer heaven, just missing gaming chairs and neon lit computers.

I have a feeling DJ may be enjoying it.

"Hm, I really hope it's not here. I would love to avoid getting framed for something I didn't do," she mutters and starts opening doors around the area. "Hm, nothing here either."

"Let's try the second basement level," I suggest, knowing that its existence is not very popularized. "You can only get to it using the stairs, so we don't have any desks there, as it's not accessible for people in wheelchairs. I don't think I've been there in years."

"Second basement? Didn't know there is one—also that doesn't sound ominous at all. You might as well say 'let me show you my murder room,'" she comments.

"Yes, it's where we bury the bodies of our enemies and plan to take over the world," I joke, but she looks like murder—pun intended.

We get to the bottom of the stairs and find an open area full of old furniture and kit, computers from 30 years ago, boxes full of wires, and equipment better off in a museum or a dump.

"Now, this is more like it!" She sighs in bizarre contentment and starts rummaging, picking up boxes, and moving the old kit from place to place, but seemingly being careful to put everything as she found it.

"This would have gone a bit faster if you would have told me what we are digging for," I point out.

"Good things come for those who wait." She smirks at me, winking. "THERE!" She screeches and pulls a sheet from over a desk and does the 'the price is right' award showing gesture.

"Here we go Jon, how your information gets out and your phone bill is through the roof... here it is... a good old... fax machine."

Indeed, a gray machine, 'fresh' design from the 90s, sits on the desk. It's clearly well maintained, with an old-style corded phone receptacle on the side.

"The sheet cover-up was a pretty silly giveaway—if I were hiding it, I would have just dropped a bunch of old laptop chargers on top of it, making it look like junk." DJ looks around the desk and checks the connections on the fax and starts to write down on her phone the previously used numbers.

"I don't suppose they would have called Miranda's home landline, but I'll get my PI to check it out," I volunteer. "I also don't suppose you could install some cameras here so we can see who our classic technology user is?"

Hearing of surveillance equipment potential, a wicked smile lights up her face. Which triggers a grin on mine and I drag her to me.

"Well, Avril, I see you are quite excited to do some spying," I murmur in her ear as I start lifting her skirt, touching her ass. DJ draws her breath in sharply as I move my hands toward the front, and run my fingers up and down her leg, getting to the apex of her thighs, where I find her wet already. "Soaked for me?"

"I've been drenched ever since you picked Princess Peach," she whispers against my neck, licking and nipping, as I continue touching her pussy, spreading her wetness over her folds, caressing her mound with my fingers.

"You want to touch my pink pearl?" She grins at me and makes me laugh. "Maybe penetrate me with your giant phallus?" Dahlia continues the trashy romance novel commentary.

"I'll give you a thorough penetration skater girl, don't worry!" And shove two fingers in her channel without warning.

DJ gasps and leans against me more, holding onto my biceps, panting as I drill her slowly, while gently biting her ear. "Also, thank you for confirming I have a giant phallus," I tell her. She shudders in laughter and moves away from me, taking the hand that was partially in her just a moment ago.

"Come on, humble romance hero, let's find somewhere less 'scene of the crime' so I can see what your phallus can do." She moves and I follow, watching the swish of her skirt as she goes up the stairs to the IT department.

She does not turn on the lights, just leads me to the couch someone brought in there, and sets me down. The fluorescence of the drink's fridge behind her lights her silhouette, and I gasp as she slowly unzips the back of her dress and lets it drop. Stepping out naked, a nymph with perfect breasts and hips made just for me, kneels down in front of me, conquering queen.

I lean forward and put my hands in her hair and let it loose, waves of darkness falling over her beautiful skin. DJ takes the helm of my shirt and lifts it, but immediately after I take it off, I lift her and set her astride on my thighs, naked pussy rubbing against my hard cock still covered by my shorts. She moves her hips over me, and I draw a nipple in my mouth, sucking it and gently grazing it with my teeth.

"Shit Jon, do that again," I get instructed and definitely have no problem following that order, feeding on her other tit, feeling her hardened peak with my lips, directing her hips with my hands to move faster as she straddles me.

Her arms on my shoulders are keeping her anchored when I lift her to lower my shorts. I manage to get my wallet and dig out a condom, break the wrapper and roll it on my erection and I guide her back down.

My breath hitches watching her sink on me, tingles and shivers all over my spine, fascinated by the shape of her body lit from the blue LEDs behind her. When I move my eyes to hers, I see the fire in DJ's brown orbs elevated into incandescence, amazement and something more, which I know she can find in my expression as well, as the beautiful woman in front of me smiles at me.

When she is fully seated on my cock, she pauses for a second, taking me in as I do her, then she brings her mouth to mine. I kiss her deeply, sparks flying between us as she starts to move on me, riding me slowly at first.

Painfully slow, moving up and down my length, she drives herself on me as I hold her, digging my fingers into her plump ass. The feeling of her hot wet cunt gliding over me is unmatchable. Breaking our kiss, Dahlia puts her hands back, holding herself on my knees, and moves faster and faster, panting. I am mesmerized by watching her slit covering my dick, glazing it with her wetness repeatedly. I circle her clit with my finger, synchronized with her runs, and I feel her breath catching as her pussy starts clenching, strangling my shaft as she peaks all over me, drenching me in her release.

But I don't stop, pulling my woman to me, holding her up with my arms and starting thrusting from below as I gently bite her shoulder, marking her as mine again.

"Again!" I command and put my middle finger on her lips. She knows what I want and opens up and starts ravishing my digit with her tongue as she would my cock, taking it deep in her mouth as my dick pounds into her.

When I think it is wet enough, I put my hand back against her ass and use the other hand to open her up, and then start massaging her other entrance with my digit.

"Oh, fuck, put it in, please, I am so close," she pleads with me, the begging I was looking for finally here. I oblige, slipping it slowly all the way into her ring, feeling her filled and tightening against me. DJ kisses me again in desperation, grazing my back with her nails, as her hard nipples slide against my chest, sweat, heat, and need between us.

I move my finger and cock in and out of her no more than a few times when she shatters, my orgasm surging as well and we come together rutting like animals in the dark, my finger in her ass, her marks on my skin, my teeth imprint on hers.

"I sure hope there were no cameras here," I manage to verbalize after a few minutes of just breathing, trying to return to this plane of existence.

"Ha! No way, the first thing I did was disable them as I don't need people recording me while I work," she confirms and kisses me briefly before getting up and going to clean up in the bathroom.

I stare at the barely visible popcorn ceiling for one minute, then manage to get up and find the restroom as DJ exits, and I drag her in for a proper kiss before I go in myself.

"Shit, that was tonight? Uh, got a bit distracted," is what I hear returning to the IT area to put my clothes back on. My woman struggling to get her zipper up while holding her phone is pretty amusing as well.

"Indeed, I got a good dicking, Lau," she rolls her eyes at me when I chuckle and mouths 'my sister' as I help her get dressed. "See you in about an hour. Yes, sorry again I am late. I will deliver coffee to you all next week. Yes, the expensive one. OK, keep your legs closed. I will be there in a bit and then you too can get laid. *Hasta luego, hermana*!"

"So, based on overhearing half the conversation, your sister is... not a nun?"

"I'll let her know you said that. Let's see if you enjoy getting punched in the balls." She smirks at me, but what this tells me is that she talked about me with her family.

"How about instead, you tell me when I can take you out on an actual date?" I ask, holding her in my arms, and kissing her neck.

"Actual date? But we already ran from angry reporters, had some family drama—while saving wildlife—, and had a mini sex marathon in between playing video games and solving the 'Mystery of the Hidden Fax'. I think you are doing pretty good. But, if you insist, I will look to see if I can find some free slots in my calendar for you," DJ says as she licks my lips, looking at me all mischievously.

"I do insist! We must promote our mini sex marathon to a full-on sex marathon," I counter, and she giggles against my t-shirt, which makes me embrace her even harder until she squeaks.

What hits me like a sack of bricks is how much I enjoy making this woman laugh. Having my arms around her. The feel of her hair against my skin, her coconut smell surrounding me. Listening to her clever retorts. To think I lost an entire week of her!

"But not tomorrow, I already have a date," she drops casually and I still, an unexpected chill going down my spine.

But quickly, my ass gets grabbed and a sultry voice in my ear, "Relax caveman—it's with a dashing ten-year-old swindler who is cashing in on his first Disney token. So, listening to bad rap from people named 'lil' something, on a few hours' drive one way in Florida traffic—with a little boy who may or may not admit to being car sick. All that, followed by a full day running from ride to ride in the sun and heat is most definitely my first choice versus a date with a funny and hot owner of a giant phallus."

As a consequence, this is how Dahlia Jara found herself flat on her back, getting tickled.

"Ah Avril, you asked for this, and you know it," I announce over the sound of her squeals. "Someone is in a jesting mood. Let's see how entertaining you think you are after a few minutes of this..."

"I yield! I yield!" she shrieks after a bit, and no sweeter words have been uttered.

I let her up to catch her breath—her face is all red from all the laughing as she fake smacks my side.

"Jackass!" DJ hisses at me but I know she isn't angry with me, as she is showcasing her smirk. "Fine, I will go out with you if you're asking so nicely."

"I think I should probably book a boxing session with my trainer as I just felt a mosquito bite on just now."

"If you drag me anywhere near a gym, mister, you will lose more than your balls. I will leave the six-packing to you while I do... literally anything but."

"Anything *butt*?" gains me a harder slap and a shake of the head.

"OK, Jon," she continues with a condescending pat, "you think of a date which does not conclude in your untimely death. While my sister searches for her 'catch of the night', I need to babysit."

"Keep Tuesday evening open if I were you," I decide for her. I thought she would have gone for the boxing, but a few more ideas pop into my mind—hopefully all of them ending with her under me. Or on top, I'm not picky. "I'll give you a lift to your house or where you left your car." I get the door for her.

"Home would be great, thank you. Let's put that sheet back on the fax before we go, though. I will come in early Monday to set up the cameras."

As we exit, I automatically take her hand in mine, making our way back to the parking lot together, feeling like the most normal thing in the world.

DJ

W ear something comfortable and no heels.

What in heaven's name was that supposed to mean? I am perfectly comfortable in my 4-inch Manolos, thank you very much. But the jerk wouldn't give me any more details. OK, not an actual jerk, but... jerk... when he doesn't tell me where we are going!

Definitely a jerk for making me spend hours picking something for this great date he has been so secretive about! Halfway through trying to get into some jeans and giving up after realizing I wasn't also going to fit into and breathe at the same time, I did wonder why I was so concerned.

He saw me naked a few times already. Why did it matter what clothes I chose? I can wear anything and look good! I told myself that confidently, and then changed a few more outfits until I found something which didn't scream I was trying too hard, but also didn't look like I picked it up from a thrift store. Just a few more outfits. OK. A LOT more, but who's complaining?

So, definitely a jerk for playing these mind games. Wear something comfortable! How is that an indication of what we are doing? I pull down on my strappy top, which has an unfortunate habit of riding up my back, not staying put over my flared pink skirt. In a way, I am glad I have my pink Converse on, as I probably would have dug a trench in my hallway with my heels from all my pacing.

Why the hell am I so nervous? I look at my phone and see Jon running 5 minutes late and ponder waiting for him outside. But that would be desperate. And I, Dahlia Jara, CEO of J-AvTech, and hard-core programmer and aerospace engineer, am definitely not that.

I jolt as I hear my doorbell, and I take a breath before I open the door. And I needed the extra oxygen boost, as Jon appears as he stepped out of a magazine. He has white shorts and a light blue shirt with sleeves rolled up, and those tats are revving up my engine like nobody's business.

"A skirt?" he quizzes me with an obvious smirk, as he is doing a survey of my outfit, from my shoes to my hair. His eyes sparkle when he notices my ponytail, and I knew that would get him reminiscing about a certain lunch.

"You said comfortable. I complied. Now—are you going to tell me where we're going?"

"I'd rather show you. But first things first." He smiles wickedly and before I can comment, pulls me into his arms and kisses me as if it's his last night on Earth. His warm body makes me lightheaded. In no time, I am only holding myself up by digging my fingers into his shirt, as our tongues brush against each other, and his hand is already fisting my ponytail.

"Shit, Avril, I have to stop, or we are not going anywhere." Jon pants as he pulls back slightly. "Come on, let's go before I find out what color panties you have under that skirt."

He waves me toward his SUV and I throw a classic, "Who says I'm wearing any?" behind my shoulder, making him grunt and putting a grin on my face.

"So, now can you tell me what we are doing?" I repeat my question as I buckle my seatbelt.

"Are you sure you are not the 10-year-old going to Disney? Or you can't be patient?"

I huff and poke him in the side before he starts the car, and he obviously just chuckles.

"Sure. Me. Patience. Same sentence." I raise my eyebrow at him as the Range Rover leaves my driveway, heading to the extra secret location.

"Is this one of those billionaire dates? Private jets and dinners on top of skyscrapers?" I quip with a sideways glare.

"It defeats the purpose if your date already has had her arm halfway in an airplane wing. As for dinner... I already have something planned, but skyscraper sounds a bit cliché."

"Ha, you are right. Last thing I need to see is the inside of a plane. Well, unless it's en-route to a Caribbean Island. In which case... my passport is back at the house. Turn the car around!"

Jon laughs at that. "Noted. I would need to check the private jet roster though; we only have one for the board members unless they bought their own."

"Only one jet... oh no.... billionaire life is hard!" my sarcasm is dripping over every word.

"You know I'm not actually a billionaire, right?" He glances over at me as the car stops at a light.

"OMG!" I say in mock panic. "Does it mean I'll have to just spend my own millions? The horror! Oh well, poor-man, I think I will survive by only eating at 2* Michelin restaurants."

"Ha-ha, what a hilarious lady I got here. Not saying I'm poor, but definitely not going to buy you Hove and put them out of business for being dicks to you."

"Darn, I was looking forward to that! That's what a true romance hero would do!"

"Darn, you drew the short straw with me. To be fair, McAv almost went bankrupt in 2008, I am lucky to still have my millions."

"Uh? Really?" I gasp at the direction change.

"Yeah... I just took over and then... the financial crisis hit. Suddenly private aviation was not such a hot commodity," he says with a sigh.

"Shit! What did you do?"

"What I could... Had to sell a lot of my dad's property to pay wages and some loans he took at a really bad interest rate. Then sold more and more stock to keep the doors open. What started with me having a controlling interest turned into me only having a small percentage and a multitude of investors having the rest. Even my CEO position is subject to a board oversight. And jet sharing."

"You weren't kidding about the board. They can just remove you?"

"Not easily," he winces. "I managed to turn the company around with some serious cost reduction while still maintaining most of our workforce." Jon pauses midway through his story. "Wow, I sound like a corporate drone!" I giggle as that was comparable to him reading it from a PR pack, and wave at him to continue. "But even recently, with the markets being as they are, I had to outsource some work—like the IT work."

"Yeah, I did find it a bit weird at first. But talking to a few of your staff, as long as they can get headphones from the equipment van and someone can install their software remotely, they didn't appear to be fussed."

"We manage. But the Board is a bit of a pain in the ass, always needing handholding and running through the profit numbers. Luckily, they are usually split into two factions who don't get along. Some of the old guard who had stock when my father was running the place and the new investors."

Jon slows down the car as he takes a left to the port sector and my palms start sweating, but still hoping he isn't taking me where I think he's heading to.

"Internal politics playing in your favor, huh? I... I'm going to ask again-where are we going?"

"Pretty much. If they could agree on anything, I could really get the boot, providing I do something really unacceptable. And no need to worry, we are here!" he declares with excitement in his voice, but when I see where he parked, I blanch.

"What's wrong?" my date asks as he opens my door, but my trainers are glued to the carpet.

"Umm... please tell me we are not going on one of... those!" I point to a giant yacht moored in a dock next to the carpark.

He frowns, obviously confused for a second, but then tries to make sense of my reaction. "Well, I didn't think to advise you to wear trousers, but I am sure the skirt in the wind will only be creating a few 'Marilyn' moments. Not that I'm going to complain."

"It's not about the skirt, caveman!" I roll my eyes. "It's... It's... on the... WATER!" I spurt as I point at the ocean.

"The... water?" Jon scowls for a second, then his face breaks out in a grin. "Don't tell me, Ms. Jara, have I found another weakness of yours... are you... afraid of... water?"

"Hmf," I puff, crossing my arms and looking anywhere but at him. "I wouldn't say I am afraid... more like... like..." I squirm a bit more in the car seat. "I... I can't swim, alright?" Lifting my eyes at him, I bite my lower lip.

"You... can't swim?" he asks skeptically. "But... we live in Florida." He points to the large water mass next to us. "Flo-ri-da! It's a peninsula! We are surrounded by water on three sides!"

"Thanks Jon, I know the geography! Just because we are Floridians doesn't mean I know types of alligators either, for fuck's sake!" I exhale slowly, pinching the bridge of my nose as the blue pond is a bit too close for my liking. "I did try swimming when I was young. My sister is a goddamn fish, can't get her out of the waves. But me... and water over my head. Or not touching the bottom? Or... OK. Just that. It's the big water... like THAT."

"You mean... the Atlantic?" He turns to where I am indicating briefly, then shakes his head in disbelief. "I am confused. Why did you say you wanted to go to a Caribbean Island?"

"Are you kidding me? Massages? Hotel sheets? Cocktails by a controlled-height pool with no waves? A resort sounds just fine. I can even sit in a lounge on the beach, provided there is enough alcohol. But I am in no way, shape or form getting on a boat."

"You know it's not a dingy, right? It's a 200ft superyacht, and it's extremely safe."

"Nope. My hands are clammy just thinking of it swaying in the waves. No way am I going in the middle of the ocean."

The man squints at me, the wrinkle in his brow visible, but then an elated smirk takes the place of his frown.

"Alright Avril, if you are not interested in donut burgers, I guess we can go."

A loud gasp from me makes him chuckle.

"How did you know?" I inquire.

"I guessed based on your junk food 'inclination', I noticed when you inhaled your pizza and when I saw what's in that fridge at work. Don't get me wrong, that little moan you did when I found those chocolate ice-creams in the freezer got me hard in an instant."

Crossing my arms, I glare at him. But as that dumb dimple is still very apparent, he knows I am impressed that he knew exactly what I wanted to eat.

"How about a compromise?" Jon tries again.

"Com-pro-mise? What foreign language is that?" I stick my tongue out like a child.

"Very funny, DJ, but that tongue is going to get you in trouble. How about we don't actually go anywhere, just go up and have dinner? The boat stays moored; I promise."

"Hmm." I stare at the white death trap behind him again. It looks pretty slick with its curved hull and modern design, and maybe it doesn't look as scary just sitting there. Maybe it is pretty stable anchored by the dock, with just a breeze about.

Maybe.

The man got me a fucking yacht date! And my donuts.

"No moving? No 'King of the World' moment?"

"Nope. Definitely no DiCaprio-ing." He shakes his head and extends his hand. "Come on, I didn't think you'd resist a good challenge."

"Just to note, based on the 'Queen Elizabeth 2' over there, and the dinner selection, this does count as a billion-aire date."

"So noted, Avril." His smirk is infuriating and if it wasn't for the ocean of doom next to us, I would do something about it. Probably I'd drag his ass in the back of the car and do a bit of a deep-sea exploration of my own to rediscover what's behind his shorts, in appreciation of the ridiculously over the top date.

He does feel the need to correct me, however, noting, "But the ship's name is 'The Flyer'."

I roll my eyes at him again over the sound of his deep laughter but allow him to take my cold palm in his ridiculously warm one, and to be gently pulled from the Range Rover.

With every step approaching the craft, my breath hitches and my blood pressure rises, and I clutch onto my date's hand harder and harder. An overwhelming sensation of dread sweeps over me as Jon steps on the boarding ramp and I freeze.

"You OK there, DJ? Look, this was a bad idea, we'll go somewhere else," he remarks, his green eyes watching over me in concern.

"Nope," I squeak. "I... I can do this." The sway of the boat is freaking me out so I turn back towards the car, but I don't want to be defeated by a dumb aluminum construction. "Distract me," I tell my date.

"Alright. Let me try one more thing and if that doesn't work, we go, OK? I don't feel right pressuring you to go up the ramp." My knees go a bit weak, hearing the caution in his tone. "Right..." Jon continues tentatively, "close your eyes."

I show him my middle finger instead, causing him to rumble my name. The familiar low voice in which he says "DJJJ" relaxes me slightly, and I chose to play nice and lower my eyelids.

Temporarily unbalanced by the loss of sight, I grab onto the rail, breathing slowly, taking in the salty air and attempt to center myself with the sound of the waves and seagulls, but the reality of having a water pit right next to me is not making things easy.

A whiff of Jon's cologne gives his position away as I can tell he moves closer to me. He moves my ponytail out of the way and his fingers leave goose bumps in their trail as he touches my skin. His nose runs over my neck, the texture of his beard following, scraping against the strap on my shoulder as he puts both his hands on my waist.

I gulp as his teeth pull on my ear lobe gently.

And gulp even more as he whispers, "Eyes closed," as he just lifts me as if I weigh nothing and only takes a few giant steps of his until he puts me down, on what I assume is the deck of his boat.

Frankly, if I wouldn't have my blood pressure going through the roof, I would have found that extremely sexy. Who am I kidding? I was already clenching my thighs together.

"Jon!" I exclaim instead and try to open my eyes but the taste of lips against mine shuts me right up. It's easy to forget all about the water surrounding us, not even knowing what planet we are on as his tongue sneaks in, dominating mine, and I need to grasp his shoulders to keep myself steady. His hands move to my ass, his digits digging into my garment.

"How hungry are you?" my caveman heaves, as he rests his forehead on mine.

"Not that hungry," comes out raspy, and I find myself moved again, this time my back touching a wall.

"Too bad," he says, and I can guess a sneaky smile pulling at his lips, "I am ravenous. But unfortunately, my attempt at distracting you may have backfired."

The thud of Jon dropping forces my eyes open, but I don't notice anything in the luxury yacht, as I have a god kneeling in front of me.

JON

O K, I didn't expect to be a horny jackass who can't keep his paws off his woman. My control snapped twice already, once when she opened the door and reminded me of cotton-candy with that flowy skirt and fucking adorable pink shoes with white shoelaces. Sporting pink lipstick and a naughty but strategical ponytail. I just had to sample her. So, I did.

I was pretty excited to rent 'The Flyer' again, as I usually take her out for a long weekend, when I want to blow off some steam and go jet skiing a bit further off the coast. But I ended up almost blowing the date right out of the water, as clearly, I miscalculated. Thank goodness for the deep-fried dough and grilled beef combo to entice DJ.

Her vulnerability was completely unexpected, so used to her kicking-ass-and-taking-names attitude. I had to restrain myself from grabbing her in a bear hug so she never had to be worried again. To put her in a cocoon and have her safe and secure, while I protect her against everything. But that isn't for my skater girl, who was close to decking me the first time I met her. Not for the force of nature which is Dahlia Jara. Hence, I chose the least 'brute'-y reaction to show her the boat is not that bad and that she can actually get on it herself.

That's when I lost it the second time. The 'distraction' technique turned out to be a swift way of distracting myself instead of the brunette. The moment I touched her soft skin, I lost the plot completely and took another taste by nibbling on her ear. Out the door went my initial plan of walking her slowly up the ramp, easing her in, and I just picked her up and had her against the wall.

"Caveman," her voice trembles and my adrenaline spikes as I put my hands on her knees and gently part her legs. The small yelp from DJ when I start lifting her skirt is similar to a gun going off at the beginning of a race, and I hold my breath as I slowly reveal more and more of her limbs, keeping myself in check instead of ripping the damn material off her.

My jaw slackens and I still when I get to the apex of her thighs. Flicking my gaze at her, I see a triumphant smirk.

"Told you so."

A celebratory growl of my own makes her brace herself by putting her palms on the wood paneling, but not before securing the skirt in the elastic, green lighting my impromptu apéritif idea.

"I am glad I didn't believe you earlier, or we would have never left your house," my snarl doesn't give her the option to respond as I put my lips on her very panty-less pussy.

Her sweet flavor floods my mouth and lap at her folds, crazy about her.

I lift one of her legs over my shoulder for better access, but quickly decide it's not enough, and that I want her fully under my control, and ignoring her gasp I hold her ass up with one hand and raise the other leg, and recommence my feast while holding her up against the wall.

"Fuck, Jon, this is too much," she cries, but I was already tasting her arousal on my tongue. My tongue circles around her clit and she moans, and looking up, I see one of her hands snuk under her top and she is touching her breast.

My cock is painfully hard, but I am not ready to let her down yet, and I suck on her nub and bring my index around her entrance, and start mindlessly pumping into her. The sounds coming out of her validate my every swipe of the tongue and graze of my beard against her inner thigh. When I add a second finger, I glance back up at her and her closed eyes and parted lips are a vision.

DJ is so responsive that I struggle to focus, just wanting to marvel at her pinching her nipple under her bra and letting me be savaged by the animal I turned into, incapable of stopping. I keep going, groaning, as every lap of her folds and pump in her pussy brings us both too close to the edge. I start remembering the Cessna service manual pages so I don't come without even getting my dick out, glad that I can tell by the staccato in her breath that she is near coming.

I help her along by adding a third finger and increasing my rhythm. The convulsions around my hand don't take long to manifest, as her channel is squeezing my digits and her juices flood my beard.

The best hors d'oeuvre in the world and I am the lucky bastard to have it. I bask in the taste of my woman, not wasting any of her savor as she quivers, and I hold her even tighter.

The tremors subside with the sound of her panting and I lower her, noticing how her head leans on the wall and her eyes remain closed. She is still living through her orgasm, and I am powerless from rising and kissing her again.

"This was a really good diversion. This boat is really stable. Me... not so much now," she whispers against my mouth.

"I am delighted you agree. Wasn't my original plan... but I can't seem to help myself around you," I admit. The knowing smirk and devilry in her eyes tell me how pleased she is about that outcome.

"One thing I am not in agreement with." She mock-pouts and I want to bite that plump lower lip. "Why are you allowed to have a starter and I am not?"

I don't even have time for my neurons to fire up when she uses the element of surprise to put me against the wall. With a Cheshire-cat smile she descends, taking my shorts and underwear along.

"I won't last long, Avril." It's my turn to wheeze as my cock juts toward her and the spectacle of DJ at my feet, licking her lips and craving me, makes my heart flutter.

"Good," she states, the glint in her eyes promising many wicked things. "Then grab my hair and use my mouth already, caveman."

My groan can be heard from the other side of town, as my woman takes me deep inside, already choking on me, tears around her eyes. I snap and do what I was told, fisting that alluring ponytail, and start driving in faster, not taking my focus off her face. The sight of my dick sliding between her lips reduces my vocabulary to—very loud—interjections and solitary vowels.

I wish I could have held on longer, the warmth and moisture of her mouth heavenly, but the moment DJ starts massaging my nuts, I surrender. Pulling on her hair harder, my shaft throbs and takes advantage of her accommodating mouth to release.

The surge of electricity from my balls to my cock connects with the rest of my body. Everything spirals out in color and light, like all synapses in my brain fire simultaneously, ruining and rebuilding me, and leaving me dumbstruck.

Depleted, my knees give out and I slide down the oak wood panel at my back. A rather smug-looking Dahlia climbs over my legs and puts her arms on my shoulders.

"Do you think it's bad we both put out on our first date?" she asks and my eyes pop open to trying to convey that it was not my intent, but the second I do, I am faced with a self-congratulatory, beaming grin, so I reconsider my response.

"I want to say that I'm upset about the development... but..." I leave it there as she is obviously not disappointed either.

"Are there any places you are afraid to go to?" DJ's expression is still playful, her nails going through my hair, scratching my skull, a million pinprick-like sensations traveling down my back.

"Mm?" Words escape me, my eyelids dropping under the unplanned head massage.

"I mean... it's only fair we work on your phobias too, isn't it?"

I open one eye and she giggles.

"I see, maybe next time you can pick the date, and see what you find," I counter.

"Oh, you are optimistic about a second date huh?" Her teasing reawakens me, reminding myself my trousers are around my ankles, and that I have a commando queen on top of me.

"What I am positive about is that you shouldn't be asking questions you already know the answer to. For example, 'is Jon getting hard again?' and 'should I sit in his lap wearing just this skirt?' are rhetorical."

"Are all these answers 'yes', by any chance?" DJ bites her lower lip, brown eyes boring into me again, this time with mischief and roguery. For the third time today, I pounce on her, flattening her against the carpet in no seconds flat.

"Groaning again, caveman?" She seems unphased, more amused than anything, enjoying provoking me.

"You make me do this, Avril, with those taunting comebacks. OK, this tank top doesn't help either, I have been meaning to unwrap you for the past half an hour."

DJ readies for a snappy retort, but it is her stomach that interrupts, a muffled growl signaling I have to attend to her other needs first.

"Come on, let's get you fed. With actual food." I have to specify, as she is already giving me side-eye.

I get us both vertical and drag my shorts up, getting my phone out to text the crew to bring our dinner over.

"Uuu staff... fancy." She winks at me and mumbles to herself, "Billionaire date, indeed".

She hesitates a bit seeing the water on our left, so I pull out a chair for her facing the town instead of the ocean.

"Curious to see what you will come up with. I must point out I am very amenable to sports." A smile tugs at my lips as I hear the expected snort when I mentioned 'sport'.

"As long as I don't have to literally partake. I am very happy as well to sit and have a beer watching you do your thing or a match of sorts, but me running around... not going to happen. I had an elliptic. And an indoor bike. Even a step." She uses her fingers to count her attempts. "They are all useful coat hangers. OK, not the step that just gathered dust. Even tried the good old 'standing desk' for a bit, but my ergonomic chair is really the best for coding."

"Got it. I'll be running by myself then. No marathons, however?"

She smirks again, knowing exactly what marathon I am referring to. "Let's have those burgers, then we can see about some more... exercise."

Her face lights up as the steward brings our plates, and the smell of grilled meat makes my mouth water. But it is my mind—and a specific body part—which wonders to our next activity as my date picks up her burger with both hands and takes a giant bite, moaning and closing her eyes in delight.

I groan again. She slaps my side, cocking an eyebrow at me. And it is already the best date I have ever had.

DJ

I hear the doorbell in the distance, but I need to finish signing these contracts for the new PR team leader I just hired.

"One moment!" I holler, but that only makes my caller more excited. Putting my glasses away and locking my computer—hard habit to beat even at home—I stumble to my front door in my flannel shorts and Berkley T-shirt, hoping it's not Jon. Though he doesn't seem to mind my 'house bum' vibe. He would definitely make fun of me while peeling my clothes off, and I instantly feel rather giddy at the prospect of seeing him chuckle at my outfit.

"Open up bitch, I brought cronuts," my sister announces herself impatiently.

"What are you doing here, Laura? Don't you have a job?"

"Don't you?" she counters, running her eyes over me in shock, me in my PJs versus her in a pantsuit.

I roll my eyes at her and get the treats from her, leading her to the kitchen, and start pouring us some coffee. As always, as if she owns the place, she throws herself on my favorite stool awaiting service. Her cane rests by the island.

"Also, when are you going to buy a throw pillow or something around here? You literally have a sofa and a TV in the living room and a bunch of boxes."

"My office is fine," I respond, knowing damn well she is right about not fully moving in. My bedroom had a bed but no end tables, and my charger sticking straight out of the socket. Good thing I have a walk-in closet or my clothes would still be packed up. But I could never do that to my shoes. Or to my dresses.

"Also, I have a wonderful job, thank you very much, Lau. One which sometimes allows me to do paperwork in my jammies. I doubt you do all your designs wearing your I-love-Hillary outfit. Now, sis... what do you want?"

"Can't an older sister just stop by and bring pastry? Fine, don't give me that look lil D—and put some milk in my coffee for fuck's sake—I came to inquire about your date the other day," she asks with a secretive smile.

"You drove all the way here for that?"

"OK, I may have been around the corner for a client... come on spill... I want to live vicariously through you." She wiggles her eyebrows at me.

"I think if we count the number of dates YOU go on, it may be the other way around." My sister is constantly meeting men, but she never goes on second dates with them. I don't even think she knows their names. She just says she wants to live her life and not get involved again after the accident in which her husband Charlie died, I am still not sure if I can or want to push her to reconsider.

"Yeah, but you actually went out with someone you like. And you have been seeing him officially for how long now—three weeks? Not going anywhere until you tell me, especially if it's another one like the sex boat."

It was circa four weeks if I were to confess, but I could feel a smile tugging at my lips thinking of our great date yesterday.

"Fine, fine... I will say just two words and then you can go back to work—leave the cronuts, though. Are you ready? The two words are... rage room!"

She laughs at me, snorting her coffee all over my counter.

"You are a couple of adorkable nerds!"

"How is a rage room nerdy? We literally blew shit up with baseball bats. Jon also impressed-slash-scared the kid at the till asking for an even bigger sledgehammer."

"I bet he had a big sledgehammer," Laura adds, winking at me, "and he did very bad things with it. And that you... blew... something"

He does, and he did... and I did. But I don't want to share with my nosy sibling.

"Lau—you need to get a life... maybe a cat. I still don't understand why this was worth a trip here. You could have just called to get snubbed." I stick my tongue at her, then have another bite of my delicious pastry.

"OK, I think you may want to sit down for this..." At least she has the good sense to look a bit remorseful during her dramatic pause. "*Mamá* accidentally heard Marcus and I talk about you and your *novio*."

I cringe, knowing exactly what was to follow. I don't cringe exactly at the thought of Jon as my boyfriend, even though we didn't specifically have the 'talk'.

"Is she going to call today, then?"

"Probably tonight. I told her you are working all day," she grins. "She will eventually ask you to invite him to lunch on a Sunday, you know."

"OH MY GOD Laura," I groan, "it's way too soon, I'll scare him off!"

"You'll scare him off or yourself?" Yoda-wannabe in front of me asks, but it is I who almost says the words backwards.

"Umm," is all that comes out.

My older sister knows me all too well sometimes. I have been enjoying my time with my caveman but have been scared of asking the Questions.

"DJ, is this about Richard? You don't think they are the same kind of man?"

"I don't know," I confess. "Richard was funny, and we got along great at the beginning as well... and look what a turd he turned out to be. I recognize I am the one who finally dragged Jon to me, and I should be a bit less unsure, but still. That is why I am trying to not go too fast. Fighting with him and then finding excuses not to be with him... was easy. Now that we are together—I am just..." I can't seem to identify the words to say out loud.

How frightening it is to be with someone again who means more than a one-night stand, who makes me all mushy when he kisses my neck, whispering how beautiful I am. With a man who made sure my favorite yogurt brand in his fridge. How terribly alarming waking up alone at night is when we don't sleep in the same bed. How petrified I am he will want less than what I found myself wanting again.

"Lil D—this is the first guy I have seen you with which puts that smile I just saw on your face when you were thinking about yesterday. That includes Richard—who wasn't even in contention. This is a bit about you acknowledging to yourself that you are 'all in' with a man again, and being unsure if he won't skip on you like your ex. Tell me, how many times a week do you see him?"

"Well, we go out a lot as neither of us cooks, but mostly we stay at his place—as mine, as you pointed out, is a bit... barren—playing video games and watching movies. Last Saturday we went through season one of the 'Line of duty' while doing fake British accents. Jon was far better than me, but I won't admit it to his face. The fucker knew it, though. Then he pretended to be Scottish for dinner, fooling the servers and talking about his family's kilt while I had to suppress bursting into laughter whenever he used 'aye lass'. But I think we have been taking it easy, really." It all comes out in one, and I didn't even realize how much I had to tell.

"Well, *hermanita*, I believe you need a dictionary—preferably one thrown at your head—if a dude spends so much time with you, it isn't casual or easy. Especially as I have seen you drooling after falling asleep at the movies. You, my idiot sister, are in a full-blown relationship. And if you talk about him like I just heard, you are more than happy to be in one, whether you want to accept it or not. Silly DJ…"

Laura gets off her stool, comes next to me and puts her arms around me. She hugs me as I just stand there as the fool I am, berating myself on how I told Jon he is a dumbass for not reading a contract when I can't see what's right in front of me.

"I will not repeat this for an audience, but you may be correct," I sigh. "But not sure if meeting everyone at Sunday lunch will not panic the shit out of him. It sure does me."

"Don't worry, I will be right again. I can give you a pass today." She obviously hears the first sentence loudest. "It's not every day my little sis finds herself a good dick to take home to momma." She lets me go and pours herself another coffee then forages my fridge for her milk, as I try to scrub THAT particular image from my mind.

"OK, but definitely not this weekend with *mamá*. I think as 'step 1' I may need to admit out loud…" I breathe in and breathe out… "I have a boyfriend. And I need to talk to him about where our relationship is."

"Well, 'step one' is admitting you have a problem," she jokes, and I roll my eyes. "And… What else about your caveman *novio*?"

"And," I ponder what to add, but I allow myself to say, "I really like him." I tap my forehead on the marble countertop as my sibling pats my back gently, chanting, "There, there, that wasn't that hard, was it?"

It wasn't.

Should it have been?

Shouldn't I just keep myself in check until I know for sure?

But I can't, as my dumb heart is all decided.

JON

I hit the floor like a sack of potatoes as Nathan's left hook blindsides me. I hear his laughter over the stars I see on the ceiling of the gym.

"You OK down there, big man? Should I fetch you a pillow? You have heard of this novelty technique of keeping your guard up when you are you know... boxing?" My friend removes his mouthguard and asks three rhetorical questions which, if I wasn't almost out of it, would normally make me deck him.

He takes his glove off and offers me a hand up, which I accept, then I take off my gloves and headgear myself.

"Your head's just not in the match today, Jon. Is this your brunette making you all gooey?"

"No, Nate, DJ and I are fine. More than fine actually—the past few weeks have been amazing; I don't recall feeling so at ease with a woman before," I tell him, but I admit more to myself—she still pushes my buttons and can't not have the last word most of the time.

And hogs the bed. And beats me at most video games except randomly WII tennis, which makes her huff until I tackle her on the living room carpet and kiss her until we both are breathless. And she laughs loudly in the middle of restaurants when I say something she thinks it's funny. Nothing makes me feel as if I can conquer the world, as making this woman laugh does.

"Then what's wrong?" my friend inquires as we get some water before packing up our kit.

"It's work actually—you know the fax we discovered? The cameras still haven't caught anyone using it. Also, I haven't seen any more movements from Miranda, no more stealing suppliers or anything—and after the bad press she got after the charity thing, there have also not been any more announcements on their software. The PI is staking out the convenience store, which has been receiving the faxes, but no movement either. Literally nobody requested the use of that machine in weeks, the owner said."

"Hmm," Nathan looks pensive. "I am surprised as it has been a few weeks now since your girlfriend installed them—has anything changed in the office since then? Has anyone left?"

I stop and think about what changed recently... I haven't modified my routine, except maybe having lunch a few days a week with Dahlia. Even Anya—who is still there for some unknown reason, despite Mike's promise to find a replacement—hasn't fucked up anything major. What has changed... My girlfriend?

"Shit!" I exclaim, realizing the reason. "It's DJ!"

"What? She is sending the faxes?" He startles.

"No, you idiot—she wasn't even there when the tire supplier left. DJ and some of her team members have been coming in a lot more—I think today is the first day she actually worked from home in the past two weeks. She says they like the 'bunker' as she calls it. The IT department is just on top of the storage room the fax is in. Which may make our spy apprehensive to sneak in when someone is there as they can only get there using the stairs... which pass right by her desk."

"Interesting—so why don't they go after hours? Or on Friday afternoons? Everyone in Kerrington must know you fix your plane then, and you said you now have your own feisty electrician going with you." Nathan makes some valid points, but unfortunately, I can answer them all.

"I have been checking timestamps versus card accesses and everybody knows it after catching some folks leaving hours early every day. We only went to the hangar once in the past couple weeks—and we went during the week-end—as they had an inspection for the Aviation Authority to prep and we were in the way. And you haven't seen how much DJ works. I work a ten-twelve-hour day most days, but I have to get her when I leave so the security guard doesn't catch her in the sweep. Or worse, to stop her from going in the parking lot at night by herself!" I shake my head, thinking about how I found a bigger workaholic than me.

One who grumbles when I tell her it's time to go home, so I just have to pick her up and carry her to her car or mine.

With that, I have another 'I am such a dummy' moment—she's faking being upset! She revels in me going all 'caveman' on her. Argh that woman! Someone is getting a smacked bottom tonight!

"That makes sense," my mate admits and stops my reverie. "But that also means that they may try something today, when you are here with me at lunch getting your ass kicked and your missus is at home."

Without touching the 'missus' comment I just him push out of the way which makes him laugh at me, then I find my phone in my gym bag to call my woman, but I notice a text from her already

The cameras got activated, I'll meet you in your office at 2 pm so you can see the video. Also, I hope you didn't get too beat up at boxing. I do not own a nurse's outfit #wink.

I hop into the shower quickly, obviously not imagining DJ in a short white dress with a stethoscope around her neck and her glasses on. Perhaps white a garter belt.

DJ

It's obviously the same day when my sister came to psychoanalyze me a ping on my phone comes through to let me know that the cameras have been triggered. I hurry to McAv's headquarters after getting dressed in something less 'couch potato', only to find Jon already behind his desk when I arrive into his office. Luckily, his EA wasn't at her post.

He sits at his massive wooden desk like a king, with a crisp white shirt, as always, without a tie, deep in thought over something on his computer. His muscles strained against the fabric, hair glowing in the sun. Jon's scowl transforms into a dazzling smile when he sees me there, and I swoon when I find him so happy to see me. The man makes my knees weak when he gets up to greet me and drags me in for a kiss, slightly fondling my ass and fisting the ponytail I now wear just to mess with him.

"Hey Avril."

"Hey caveman."

He releases his grasp of my hair—he loves to run his fingers through my hair as I do through his—and pecks my nose.

"Before we begin, let me call Mike in. I want her involved now that we have a culprit."

"Sure thing, I'll just set my laptop up." I agree and start plugging in, when the VP walks in, as dapper as always in a black dress, with a shiny necklace matching her short silver hair.

"Hey Jon, you wanted to shave a chat? Oh Dahlia, you are back in the office? I thought you were out for the day?" she asks, a bit surprised to see me. I too am a bit surprised to see her keeping track of my location.

"Yes, Mike. DJ and I have something to tell you. Well, two things actually. But I think we will now finally find how Lex Aviation has been stealing our data."

Two things? Unsure what the second thing is, I decide to just start the video... Jon is perched on the edge of his desk, Ms. Jones stiffly sitting down on one of the chairs, with a severe look on her face.

The camera kicks off once a figure enters the room, holding a folder to their chest. The camera doesn't show the face, but we could see she is probably female based on the person's stature. They move straight to the corner with the fax, take the sheet off and start dialing a number. The machine slowly starts to go through each page, sending the information.

"This will carry on a bit as it takes about a minute a page to send a fax—that is why you had such a high phone bill. Just now they sent about fifty pages," I interrupt the recording. "But if we move on around here..."

The person in the video fidgets next to the fax, humming a sad song, then glances towards the entrance, checking if anyone sees her. And that's when I pause the video again and we can all see who it is as clear as day.

"Son of a bitch!" Jon exclaims. "It was her all along! Fuck, she had access to everything!" He paces, clenching his fists, and I am not sure what to do with the VP there. If it was just us, I would go calm him down. Switching my interest over to her, however, I can just see her stunned in her seat, speechless.

"I am going to get her now, before she sends any more of my data over." He walks over and slams the door open, and I hear a yelp from the desk next to it.

"Anya, get the fuck in here!" he yells at his EA, fuming.

Anya? The name sounds familiar and for a change, I notice her in a bit more detail. She comes in holding her middle, eyes down, mousy and small, her thick glasses on, wearing again a nondescript cardigan and gray slacks. Dark-blonde hair in a low bun. You would think she is a quiet librarian.

Jon has told me about her incompetence and all the issues he had with her, but I was never in the room with her for more than a minute or so. I wondered why she would scurry off whenever I came to visit, but never raised it with him.

My... boyfriend... points her to sit in the other chair and plants the laptop on the desk so she can see for herself.

"What do you have to say to this, Anya? How long have you been stealing information for Miranda?"

The girl is frozen, the image clearly having her red-handed. But suddenly, I observe her squaring her shoulders, putting her hands on the sides of the chair. Her posture changes as she crosses her legs, and now she appears confident and strong. Her black eyes are moving between the three of us, this time full of fire and power.

"Guess you caught me, right? So sad. Also, very sad you can't use that against me." She smirks, looking down at us like we are here for her, not the other way around. "Under Florida status 934.03 it is illegal to audio record someone without their permission—and from what I can hear in this video, that is a fax making quite a lot of noise. I am also humming next to it. Next time, try to take visual only surveillance. Or, even better, make sure I actually signed the document where I agreed to be monitored at work, audio or visual or otherwise. Maybe also check I don't have an exception filed where I am permitted not to be recorded in any capacity at work, inked by both the CEO and the VP."

"What the fuck do you mean?" Jon loses it. "What documents?"

"The ones you both signed, of course. Which you clearly both read," Anya smiles at us like the villain that she is. A well-prepared villain with extensive knowledge of laws, and how to go around them. And that is when it hits me.

"Anya... Peterson?" I ask and the two directors turn to me, confused by the question.

"Yes, that is my name," she admits, but looks less smug.

"Oh my, you are her! She went to law school with my brother! You finished the top of your class. Marcus described you as one of the smartest, most hardworking people he had ever met. What the hell are you doing pretending to be an executive assistant while selling corporate secrets?"

"Your brother is an attorney? I thought he was a tailor. I did hire her because of her degree, but she said she wanted experience in an actual company before going into corporate law." Jon is even more puzzled, while Anya sighs, gazing out the window, at least a bit contrite.

"He really is a lawyer, but he prefers making clothes, so that's what he does." I shrug, still staring at the blonde. It made more sense now why she was avoiding me; I remember her from Marcus's graduation. "Well—do you want to say anything?" I pressure her.

"If I may or may not have sent any documents—for which you don't have any usable evidence—it was not for money. For your information, why I am here is none of your business." She continues to look out the window, avoiding us.

"What do you mean, it isn't our business? It's all it is—my business! What did Miranda promise you if not cash? A new job? A career?"

"Nothing you would understand, Jon," she glares at him. "Now, are we done here? I will go clear out my desk." She simply gets up to just walk out.

I post myself in front of the door. I am only barely taller than her, but I can't just let her walk out.

"I think we need to call the police," Ms. Jones says finally, after almost not even being in the room until now. "She may be right about the recording, but I am sure if they dig hard enough, they will find something about her. And girl," she continues with a chilling voice which scares me as well, "you know they will find something. So how about you tell us how to get Miranda for this instead of you, and maybe we can make a deal?"

I watch the young woman as Mike speaks, and I notice her confidence wavering, and she winces towards the end when she hears the Lex Aviation CEO's name. Crossing her arms again, she turns directly to the VP.

"Is that right... Ms. Jones? A lot of good can indeed come from digging if you want." I glance at the older lady and she is stone-faced, angry almost.

"But you are correct," Anya continues after a breath. "All parties here would rather the police not get involved—how would it look to your board if your EA was allegedly sending documents to your bigger competitor? So, if you want me to help you with *Miranda*," she punctuates the name, "I can make sure you get an anonymous email with all I know."

"You do that now before you get the fuck out of my company," Jon concludes. "I will have a security guard shadow you before you leave, and I don't wish to see your face here ever again." He picks up the phone and calls security, while I continue to observe the ex-assistant. She is regarding the three of us quietly, and I want to ask her more about why she did what she did.

When the guard knocks on the door before I manage to form some better questions, and escorts her outside, where she sits down and starts writing.

"Well, that was exciting," Mike summarizes and walks herself over to the bar in a corner of Jon's office to pour herself a whiskey.

"It was indeed," I agree, and move closer to Jon, who looks down, with his palms on his desk, knuckles white, clearly struggling not to throw something across the room. "Are you OK, caveman?" I say soothingly. "You want to go back to the rage room? Maybe this time you can use the ax?" I put my palm on the desk next to his, and gently caress him with my pinkie.

"Yes Avril, I am this close to finding an ax right now." He lifts his head at least and takes my hand in his. "I can't believe how oblivious I was—all her incompetence was a trick—she was just pretending to be an idiot while stealing and sabotaging me."

"She was, but we caught her, OK? And what she's sending will help you bury Miranda. You need to read your contracts though," I tease at the end, seeing a small smile tugging at his lips; still not enough for the dimple to make an appearance, but it's a step forward, out of this downward spiral he seems to be in.

"I hope so—probably anything Anya sends won't hold up in court, but I am certain I can use it for something."

"I know you will. We will dig a little deeper and kick her ass. Should be easier now that she won't have a spy here."

"She won't know what hit her, uh?" he repeats what he said a few weeks back in the hangar. But unlike that Friday, he doesn't retreat, but he pulls me to him, putting his arms around me. I am enveloped in his warmth and the smell of him, making me realize all those insecure thoughts were for nothing. This man wants and needs me as much as I do him, and comparing him to anything in my past is ridiculous. I hold him around his waist and feel his breath of relief on my shoulder, as though holding me right now is all that matters.

"Ahem." We hear a cough from the room. Michaela! We forgot about her being in the office. I try to break away, but don't get far as Jon keeps me to his side.

"So, is this the second thing you wanted to talk to me about?" she asks, waving her hand between us.

"Yes, actually," he answers, giving me a squeeze. "DJ and I... well... we are together." He looks down at me like he, too, is anxious about whether I will confirm or not. Jon is worried as well about me if I am in this as well. The hope and fear in his eyes break away any and all doubts I have been struggling with. Which makes me smile with all my heart, squeezing him back.

Yes, caveman, I am all in. Please don't break my heart.

"Yes. We are," I admit to myself, more than anyone. "Please tell us if we need to sign anything."

"Wonderful!" she grins at us—phew. "Thought there was something there when you had that first meeting. Glad it all worked out." Ms. Jones moves to go back to her office, eyeing the security guard and the ex-assistant in her cubicle. "I will send the HR form over. I know you are not technically an employee, but I'd rather have the workplace relationship disclosure form in the books, just in case. Congrats again. Oh, and please don't screw on my desk," she says as a leaving salvo.

At that, Jon bursts into laughter.

"What's so funny?"

"Well, that interview in her office... I thought I would do just that," he sheepishly confesses.

"Oh, did you? What exactly did you imagine doing?" I beam.

"I swear by showing instead of talking, girlfriend." He pulls me to him as I giggle, but just then Anya knocks on the door frame.

"All done. It's in your inbox—and only yours, Jon. I also added some more interesting titbits, whether you chose to look them over or not, all on you. I know you don't believe me right now, but I am sorry. I tried to make it better where I could," she states, nodding at me, then turns around and walks out, carrying her box of personal items and being trailed by the security guard.

"What exactly did that mean?" I ask, troubled by the whole mid-afternoon.

"No idea, it's all bizarre—she seems very calm, like she was expecting to be caught—and it only took her fifteen minutes to send everything over? She must have been prepping for this from the beginning," Jon comments.

"Now that sounds more like the girl Marcus was telling me about—driven, decisive, smart. I think you kept over-looking her because she was pretending to be a lost wall-flower when she was more of a wolf in sheep's clothing."

"Indeed, I was. I can't trust myself right now, not when she made me sign a form that excluded her from recording.

I need to get better at legal forms, not just leave it all to Mike, especially after what happened with your contract, and now this." He walks over and closes the door to his office, then sits down on his massive leather chair and pulls me in his lap.

"Jon, you wouldn't have lasted for years as CEO if people would have been giving you false forms to sign. Ms. Jones has that as the main task, after all. Frankly, you aren't supposed to read every contract with every low-level company like mine, and if it wasn't for... us... it shouldn't have come up. As for Anya's form... she probably had a million opportunities to make you sign it. Even if she didn't by any chance fake your signature, she could have hidden the page in some of the many contracts you signed. She must have done the same with your VP." I reassure him as I run my fingers through his hair, feeling him relax under my touch. I love snuggling with him, his massive frame cocooning me, one of his hands on my hip and the other on my thigh, holding me sideways on his lap.

"I sure do hope so, DJ. I want to read it all, and then send it to my lawyer and private investigator to agree on how to proceed. But first, I want to talk to you about earlier. I probably should have discussed it before springing it on you, but Mike has been with my family for years, didn't feel right not telling her about us."

I can see it again, the remains of his recent concern in his eyes, worried he pushed me too fast when the one which needed pushing was me.

"In a way, I am glad you did it like this. I was a bit skittish myself earlier, and now—I don't know... am happier to be with you knowing we are out in the open."

"Yeah?" His smile dazzles me once more, and I bring my mouth to his gently, holding his face in my palms, the prickle of his beard on my skin spurring me on, kissing him harder. He touches my hair, his tongue slipping against mine, moving with purpose, as his other hand goes up my skirt.

"Yeah," I whisper before letting out a moan as his fingers brush against my panties, massaging my center over my underwear. The circles Jon makes with his tongue are synchronized with the ones he makes on the fabric covering my folds, and it's driving me crazy with need. I gasp as his middle digit goes behind the lace and finds me wet, teasing my entrance.

"Damn right," he says brusquely, and I find myself on his desk, keyboard thrown on the floor. He kneels in front of me, opening my legs.

With no more delays, he licks me, still over my underwear, sucking me and playing with me.

"Jon, I want you," I pant.

"You want me, DJ? You want my tongue on this sweet pussy? Or do you want my finger deep inside you?" he hums, looking at me with his green eyes full of desire.

"All.... All of it," I mutter, the expectation killing me.

"Then you shall have it. Then I will have all of you."

I can't answer as Jon moves my panties aside and starts ravenously licking my clit like a man starved. His finger pumps at me as he works my sex, and I am delirious with the yearning for more. I manage to hold myself up, watching him eat me up, and with every swipe of his tongue and every thrust of his digit, my breath hikes more and more.

I urge him on, calling his name, and I feel myself near, knowing a touch of him would set me off. And then the fucker just stops, pulls away, grinning at me again, beard wet with my juices.

"Oh no, Avril, I want to get you coming all over my cock, squeezing the life out of me."

"Jackass!" I scowl at him, but he is already up, unbuckling his trousers, his proud dick out and ready for me. He pushes me down, my back on his desk, spread out to him. I hear the condom wrapper and then I can feel the tip against my slit, pushing in and then stopping halfway.

"What the f..." I do not get to finish the sentence as he plunges all the way in and I go over the edge, coming like crazy, clenching my inner muscles and losing all control. Jon kisses me, barely blocking my screams from alerting the entire office.

As I start going down from my high, he starts pumping again, slowly at first, then increasing the cadence, until we shake the whole desk with his movements.

"Hell yeah, that was so good, DJ, clasping me like a vise. You are so slick. I just want to fuck you all day, to stretch you taking me all in," he says as he runs his thumb over my lip.

"Go caveman, fuck me, I need you deep inside me... Just you."

"Fuck yes!" is followed by a crescendo of thrusts, as I start sucking on his digit, nipping and licking him as Jon

188

sinks his length in, and I am building my orgasm up again, feeling waves of pleasure rising.

It hits me again, an explosion lighting my spine. Endless, indescribable thrill. Jon's growl rumbles, and I feel his cock surging in me, throbbing as he comes too, struggling to keep his groans contained.

"Hey Avril," he kisses my forehead, still in me.

"Hey caveman," I murmur in my pliable state.

We are both fully dressed, and it made what we did so much hotter, of course, I realize as I watch his tight ass walk away, going to get rid of the condom in his private bathroom. I rise off his desk and stumble into the restroom myself after he exits. When I glance in the mirror, I see not just my 'just fucked' hair and blush, but also a dumb, big, unmistakable smile.

"This is a very good look on you." My man seems to enjoy my disheveled appearance as he leans on the door frame surveying his 'work'.

"I am glad YOU like it, but I need to get this..." I say, pointing at my hair, "a bit under control before walking out. I have to go downstairs and finish checking the latest graphics my team sent over the other day."

"Mmm, would these visuals be the ones with the up-dates in colors I asked for? The ones you denied needing changing as I quote 'there's more than enough contrast, we don't need the numbers in yellow!' when I inquired why the air pressure values were barely visible and sug-gested we use the easiest-to-see color for a human eye for something so critical?" he asks with a sneaky grin as he moves closer to me then nudges his nose up and down my neck, enjoying the goose bumps I get every time he does that.

I swear the man can smell a weak spot a mile away!

"Nope, I don't recall that conversation at all. You must be imagining it," I deny between breaths, but he knows he was right.

"I see. I must have indeed imagined it, silly me." He gives me one last kiss before we go back to our jobs, not mentioning the graphics again.

As Jon lets me win this one, when he could be rubbing my face in it, I decide it is time to truly meet him halfway in jumping off the cliff together.

JON

I t feels incredible to have the weight of the sabotage
behind me. Ever since I fired Anya, there have been no
more rumblings of suppliers leaving. I even sat down with
every CEO of each company working with me in the past
two weeks to try to review their contracts and understand
their needs.

I haven't yet opened the other folder she sent me called
'ideas', unsure why, but I can't reconcile the barely passable
assistant with the confident person we saw the other day,
and I am still processing.

I did eagerly open what she forwarded me on shrew—a
damaging email chain from Anya's personal account
where she got requests for information from a random
email address. There was also an audio recording in which
I recognized Miranda's hushed voice inquiring about
which supplier is unhappy with us, and how much she

should bribe them with, in conversation with my former assistant.

What really made my attorney happy were the pictures of the guy who picked up the latest fax from the convenience store and Miranda together. There are clear images taken by my PI of him handing her over documents at a restaurant nearby. Unfortunately, as with the recordings that did not have two-party consent, the photos would not stand up in court, as we can't show that the papers my former stepmother received are the same as the ones that were faxed.

But what my lawyer set up for Tuesday night is more of a private meeting with Miranda and Ramsay on a subject which matters more to me than my company—Tabitha. He thinks the scare of a press release and bad publicity would make them agree to partial custody, at least. Perhaps seeing what his wife has been up to will also force Lexington to rein her in a bit, as it's his name and reputation she is tarnishing.

However, now I have another critical 'meeting' I am quite anxious about. Unsure why, as I have met parents of previous girlfriends before, but somehow, I am like a kid trying to make a good impression in a new school. It is probably because I was an only child growing up and there are three of them, and they have years of banding together against a common target. It doesn't help that I have a small circle of friends. Circle may be optimistic. It's just Nathan, really, and maybe Mike at times.

So, I brought reinforcements, and as Tae steps out of her Uber looking cheerful, I feel I can take on the Jara clan... at brunch.

"Hey big brother, how is it you are still so tall?" my sister teases as I get up, give her a kiss on her cheek, then pull a chair out for her. Her hair is up and she is wearing some loose overalls, making her look far younger than she is, reminding me lot of the times she was a little girl running around.

"Tall? He's like a f... fudge-ing tree!" I hear a woman's voice behind me. "Lil D you forgot to say you are literally dating a Hemsworth brother! Or was it a Skarsgård brother?"

"He is hot I give you that, but let's not compare him to a Hemsworth, or he'll get too smug," my girlfriend intervenes, and I roll my eyes at her as she gives me a PG13 kiss and starts doing the introductions. She is as stunning as ever even in a Blink82 t-shirt, with her curves on display in those black skinny ripped jeans which will grace my bedroom floor later.

"This one," she points at a tall brunette with red ends wearing a red pantsuit and leaning on a black cane, "is Laura, my older sister, and overall blabbermouth. You already met Marcus, and this is Tabitha, Jon's younger sibling, and, as you can already see, a future heartbreaker." My sister blushes and my woman goes and hugs Tae, which makes me appreciate her even more.

We all shake hands and although the brother glares at me enough that he has to get elbowed by DJ, we manage to sit down and order our drinks.

"Well, how about this sibling outing?" Laura appears to be the extrovert conversation maker. "So, Tabitha, DJ tells me you just moved to Florida—did you do it to torment Jon with endless conversations on boys and fashion?"

"Definitely the only reason," Tae deadpans, causing the Jaras to start laughing. "My mom moved back here for work, but I am glad I can see my brother more now. My new school is so much better than my old one."

"Yeah, from what you said the other day, the girls were a bit spoiled," Dahlia comments as I touch her knee under the table and I get a raised eyebrow. She knows she is irresistible to me when I can reach her skin, in this case through the tears in her denims.

"Jon," Marcus pipes up, changing the subject, "tell us a little more about yourself, besides running an aviation company—like how long was your last relationship?"

"Oh, here we go," the older Jara mutters. "*Hermanito*, you could at least let us have a drink—or three—before you start interrogating the man. We apologize, Jon. My brother thinks he's our dad nowadays. He forgets I literally changed his diapers, and that DJ read him to sleep."

"Don't worry about it," I chuckle. "I can take a grilling, and I would also expect to slow roast any guy who even looks at Tae. Maybe show him my gun collection—once I get one."

"Jon! No way!" my sister gasps, but I see Marcus looking a bit less stabby, slowly measuring me up. I knew after that conversation in the shop he wasn't going to be my biggest fan, but I respect him for trying to protect his sisters, so I can only tell him the truth.

"But now you ask, my last relationship lasted about three months, but we weren't right for each other."

"Yeah, as she wasn't old enough to buy a drink in a bar," DJ whispers for my ears alone but continues out loud for the families, "met her, lovely girl, nice shade of orange."

Laura and Tae giggle behind their glasses while I pinch Dahlia's side, and she squeals and pinches me in return, but I laugh at her.

"She who dresses like an early 2000s skater should not be throwing the first stone." I give her a pointed look, reminding her of her own fashion choices.

"Oh my word, that was that one time! I may also recall you weren't that... upset," my girlfriend throws back and her brother's face turns a bit yellow.

"Uh, DJ was a skater?" Tae asks curiously, completely oblivious to the innuendos.

"Not so much a skater, but she had to wear some old clothes. That is the first time these two met, from what I understand," Laura fills them in. "And 'meet' they have," she continues in a lower voice, clarifying that both of the relatives know what happened in the shop. Just hoping they haven't read her mother in or that will be an awkward meeting.

"Moving on!" Marcus saves the day just as our drinks are brought over. The woman in red downs half her gin and tonic as the rest of us start sipping at our beers and Tabitha has a virgin mojito.

As everyone knows attack is an excellent form of defense, I attempt interacting with DJ's brother, hoping he will stop sending evil vibes, or at least just send less of them.

195

"So, Marcus, how is the shop going? Any big orders, or is it all individual customers?"

"Actually, I have some news on that—I got an order for new suits from the Kerrington Typhoons—our local football team. They want me to make custom outfits for all their players!"

Oh's and *ah*'s from all the ladies and a 'congrats, man' from me appeases him even more. He is proud of his store and recalling the quality of his work, he has reason to be. Even the shirt and vest he has on now, in a deep burgundy with golden buttons, showcase his style and skill beautifully.

"I know it's not easy to run your own business, but it is a great acknowledgment of your technique to get an NFL team to employ you—congrats again, well deserved." I give him some honest praise and he nods at me, a level less combative. I feel a squeeze of my hand under the table from the lady next to me, and the validation that I said the right thing fills me with warmth.

"There you go with those fancy words." My girlfriend may be doing her best to make fun of me, but she secretly cherishes it. I may or may not be using more and more of them just to get scolded and see that cute pout on her face.

Conversation flows freely after that, from DJs progress with her software—she thinks her staff will finish the reconstruction in a week or two so we can start testing the predictions against real world flights—to Tae's stories about her volunteering with the local wildlife charity.

I make everyone laugh by recounting how I ended up knocked out by DJ during our WII Boxing session last night, my actual training was no match for her angry little punches at thin air.

The best part of the day is the small touches I get from my Avril. She either holds my hand or her leg rubs against mine. Putting my arm around her chair, and she leans against me when her sister tells an amusing story about her son, the coconutty smell of her shampoo delighting me as always.

I automatically kiss the side of her head before I collect the olives she hates from her salad and move them onto my plate without asking. It's then when I spot her brother looking at me and giving me a chin up 'OK, man' sign and as I raise my glass to him, and I feel like I triumphed. I realize also how at ease I am with DJ's family. I can... just be... with them and Tae.

Just as Laura tells us of her latest submission to the Miami interior design awards, a grating voice interrupts our meal and, as I turn to the entrance, my mood sours.

"Here you are, Tabitha!" Miranda marches into the restaurant straight to our table, clearly enraged and seeming a bit out of control.

"Tae?" I ask, confused as the Jara family watches, perplexed as well.

"Uh, sorry Jon." My sister looks down, adding, "I didn't tell her I was with you. I lied and said I was at the movies because I wasn't allowed to see you."

"Oh Tae." I sigh, and I am about to apologize to Miranda—of all things—when my ex-stepmother grips my sister's arm pulling her up and a gasp of pain from my younger sister makes both DJ and I jump out of our chairs.

"Hey, you can't just grab her like that," I gnarl at her. "I think you and I need a serious conversation right now!" I then turn to DJ. "Mind staying with Tabitha for a bit?"

"Not at all. Go ahead. Miranda, you better let her go right now or I will release the video from this restaurant directly to TMZ, let's see how you like that celebrity spotting." My girlfriend posts herself between them, peeling her fingers from my sisters' arms and pulling Tabitha behind her, staring up at a stunned Miranda, ready to take her down if necessary.

"I am coming with you," Marcus rises. "You know, as your lawyer."

I nod, surprised at his offer of help, but I recognize it won't hurt having a witness with me, especially one which can stop me from saying anything I shouldn't. I gaze at Dahlia, who gives me a confident smile, expressing without words that she will take care of business on her end, and I can just go handle the 'mother of the year'.

"Lawyer?" The evil witch is appalled as we step out into the foyer. "Now your attorney knows your little *puta* girlfriend as well?"

Marcus chokes on his words and is about to move toward her, but I stop him shaking my head at him and whisper, "Not worth it," thinking how half my time is spent stopping Jara's siblings from decking my enemy. I am not upset at all, though my dad's widow should know better than to start her conversations with a racial insult.

"You may want to reconsider what you suggest about the man's sister or my girlfriend," I say in my threatening CEO low voice. I observe Miranda twitching, more insecure than when she stormed in. "Now, I thought we could wait until Tuesday, but you should receive papers tomorrow requesting a change of custody arrangements. I agree Tae shouldn't have lied about where she was going, but I won't tolerate you putting your hand on her. With so many witnesses, I would love to see how you will wiggle your way out of this one."

"What?"

"Yes, Miranda, you are done. I will also show your husband how you do business with spies in my company. We have photos and audio of what you did with Anya, so I recommend you go home and start packing a bag for Tabitha. She will be coming with me tonight and we will stop by tomorrow to pick up some of her clothes until Ramsay and I can agree on a better plan." The words escape my mouth, but having formed them, I recognize that is what I needed to say for a while.

Even before the luncheon, I knew in my bones I had to take care of my family and that the Lexingtons are not the best fit for Tae. She doesn't realize that being ignored, treated as an accessory and being raised by nannies isn't normal, but after seeing how much worse it actually is in the past few weeks, I will go to the mat for her so she can have a better adolescence.

"You have no right to take her!" she shrieks. "I have custody!"

"Lady, she's either going with Jon or I am calling the police and Child Protective Services. I personally know a judge who will not just hand Tae over to him, but will supply you with a nice orange jumpsuit. It works with

your skin tone, I agree, but I don't think you want that."
DJ's brother next to me shuts her up, making me extremely appreciative he came with me.

I can see her seething, about to throw a giant tantrum, but then she looks behind me at DJ and Tae inside and smirks, giving me the chills.

"Fine Jon, take her tonight, but mark my words, you won't have her for long. I wouldn't get too attached to your girlfriend either, I will make sure neither of you gets what you want." Miranda gives us a middle finger then turns and walks out, without even saying goodbye to her daughter. I can't believe she just left, leaving us with half-assed threats.

"Shit... what was that about? She backed away too quickly," Marcus voices my thoughts.

"No idea, man. She must have something else up her sleeve, but I do not know what. Come, I need another drink before I get the girls home in a taxi."

"I will join you, and I suspect my sisters will down several as well. So—are you ready to raise a teenager?" He grins at me.

"Not in the slightest, but she is my sister. I have to take care of her," I answer honestly, the reality of what I am about to do hitting me straight in the face. I always wanted to spend more time with Tae, but I need to step up fully now. Fuck—I will get it done for her. I just hope I don't mess it up.

"That's why I now can see how you are good for Dahlia. If you love and take care of your family, you will care for my sister as well. Even though it scares the shit out of you."

He man-pats my back and returns to our table, leaving me staring after him.

I am indeed scared shitless, as Marcus adequately put it. But I have my sister now with me instead of worrying about her with Miranda and I also have DJ.

Because when I said take the girls home, I meant both 'my' girls, as I don't just care about Tae, I care about Dahlia Jara. My fearless and funny and often silly woman, which I care for more than I should after such a short time. But I do and decide right there and then I will not be letting her go, and pray she won't either.

JON

I knock softly on the door frame and Tae lifts her head from her phone.

"Hey sis, how do you like the room?"

My guestroom is probably the least appealing place in the house, as it's usually used by Nate sleeping off a night of heavy drinking or, once in a blue moon, by my mother when she visits from the South of France. So, it's basically a bed and a couple of side tables with an empty wardrobe.

"It's... a room. But I can make it better. I have some ideas—did you know 'very peri' is the color of the year?" She smiles with intent, and I will definitely need to hire an interior designer and some builders, as DIY is definitely not a skill of mine. And google veri peri! I hope it's not neon green.

"That sounds... interesting. By the way, DJ called her personal shopper to pick up some clothes and toiletries for you and will bring them over in a bit."

"She did? Awesome! Are there any NA-KD in there? Any Lululemon?" She eyes her overalls, which clearly weren't a long-term plan.

Marcus didn't even scratch the surface. Scared shitless doesn't begin to cover being faced with girls' clothing brands. Unsure if those were clothing brands, could be perfumes for all I know.

"I think that's a question for DJ." I sigh and sit on her bed. "There is something else I want to talk to you." I pause a bit, as it isn't an easy subject, and try to find my words. "It's about what happened earlier with your mom. I wanted to know if she ever did anything like that before?"

"God, Jon! No!" she declares, and by the look on her face, I see she is telling the truth. "She never did. She never grabbed me or hurt me. I think the whole move here stressed her out. We usually do Saturday shopping sprees, or we go to the spa, but ever since we came here, she has been in the office day and night. I know you two don't get along, but we do spend time together and some days she really tries to do the right thing, and involve me in her life. The problem is that besides clothing, we don't have that much in common."

"OK, Tae, I trust you. But you do realize she should be more involved in your life, not the other way around, right?"

"I am aware. But that's just not who she is. She doesn't understand me fully, and I don't really get her. I didn't want to tell you, but I have been a bit lonely ever since Mia, my former nanny, retired."

"Why didn't you say? I could have called more. Or done more Zooms? I would have flown over to New York more, too." Shit, have I been messing up for a while? The memory of calling me the day I met DJ hits me, and I am ashamed I fobbed her off so quickly, when my sister clearly needed me.

"I... don't know. Maybe I should have been more honest." Tabitha looks sad, and I am at a loss for what I can say or do to make it better.

"But Jon, it's OK, I am here now. Thank you for letting me come home with you. I was a bit worried at the restaurant and was not sure I should leave my mom's, but now that I am here, I feel much better."

"Nonsense. You are always welcome here. Maybe I could have painted the room before though," I change the subject as I am beginning to really worry. I will fuck this up.

"Yes, white is boring," she giggles. "I have ideas. I'm going to make a Pinterest board and show you!"

"OK, that sounds like a great plan." It should keep her busy for a while. "If you want to come down in a bit, food is coming."

"Chinese?" Her eyes sparkle at the thought of sweet and sour chicken.

"Always, for you."

"YES!" she whoops, and I am glad I can get at least dinner right.

DJ

The family brunch I had planned to introduce gently Jon to my siblings went a bit 'Pete tong' and yet somehow Miranda's meltdown brought us all together more than a few drinks did. After the witch left, we all made sure Jon's sister was OK, and then sat around the restaurant for another round, mostly bitching about what we all witnessed.

Marcus also warmed up to my boyfriend even making some 'man2man' jokes. Laura was already his supporter. Meeting him only confirmed it, with a wink and "good job" as she pinged my ear on her way out, in her annoying 'big sister' kind of way.

Jon was a bit stunned and anxious, fingers rapping on the table until I held his hand in mine, but he did try not to show his sister that he, too, was not expecting the whole circus.

I so wish Miranda wouldn't have harmed Tae. My anger was beyond anything I experienced in a long time. I just wanted to protect that young woman and am glad Jon and Marcus took her outside before I did something truly violent.

I have been texting with Tabitha ever since the charity luncheon. I am already feeling close to her, connected by our preference for expensive shoes and clothes, and Grey's anatomy—though we both agree that the show has over-stayed its welcome. And our connection through Jon.

The stories about him would have surprised me a month ago. Now, when I hear a tale of him trying to find her a Monster doll in 2016 and calling the manufacturer's CEO himself and swapping flying lessons for a puppet for her just cements how much he loves her. How he was the only person in her life who not only asked how her studies were, but also if she was happy. If she was worried about her biology presentation that was due the next day and wanted to talk about it, not only what grade she got.

So, when we took her home that afternoon, Jon set her up in his guest room, where she seems to be settling in just fine.

Tae fell asleep early in the evening after demolishing her takeout, and I came back downstairs to find my probably freaking-the-fuck-out boyfriend.

"Hey how are you, you OK?" I ask as I put my arms around him as he overlooks the night lights over Kerring-ton from his favorite place, leaning over the railing on the kitchen terrace.

"Fuck if I know," he sighs deeply, turns then pulls me in, asking without words if I can just give him my strength, my manly man overwhelmed by the magnitude of change in his life right now. He holds me tight; I can feel his nose in the crook of my neck, touching my skin and taking refuge.

"I don't know what I am doing with Tae—I can't think what to even do tomorrow with her—take her to school? I don't have any of her books or anything... What if Miranda sends the police over tonight and says I kidnapped her? I wouldn't put it past her. And what the hell is veri peri?"

"What we are going to do is put the leftovers in the fridge as we will have them for lunch, then have a shower and relax. No, I also don't have a clue what that stupid color is, but my sister will know. You have Tabitha here, which is what you have been trying to do for years. I wish it would have been under better circumstances, but you got this. We can stop by Miranda's house on route to the school and pick up what she needs. I doubt very much she will be sending any officers after the text I sent her with the video from the restaurant as a warning." I smile, and I feel him loosen with every sentence I say. After listening to my last one, he moves back and looks at me in wonderment.

"You actually got a recording? I thought you were bluffing; didn't think they had cameras inside! Jesus, woman! You are amazing!" He picks me up and twirls me on the deck under the stars and I giggle like I'm demented, all the while loving his body holding mine, and the sound of his gleeful laughter.

"Alright, alright. Put me down, you deranged caveman."

"Nah Avril, you are all mine now, not going anywhere."
He squeezes me even more, and I can't deny his statement.

"Wasn't planning to, dumbass. No getting rid of me," I
add, and I mean every word.

"Good, you are not getting rid of me either," Jon says,
but as he lowers me and we look at each other, it is our
wordless connection, the magnetic pull between us which
flares. Here in the quiet, with no distractions, no work or
spies or relatives, just his green eyes staring into mine, chest
to chest and heartbeat to heartbeat.

There is an unspoken truth between us, the 'more'
which isn't so abstract anymore. It is days of bickering
over graphics of my software or wiring on his Cessna. It
is him holding me at night before I take over the bed.
And him sending his sister silly memes she rolls her eyes
at. It is getting tickled over computer games and wearing
his favorite shirts around the kitchen. Nights of feasting
on each other, sweat and heat and moans, the taste of his
tattoos and my hands pressing against his headboard. His
kiss. My touch.

The 'more' is me and him and us, and the words we want
to speak. Words are so insane to say with our histories,
but they are there. Palpable in the air, as the bridge built
between us. We know them, we breathe them. We act on
them as Jon kisses me softly, swaying us in a dance in the
dark.

He carries me up the stairs in silence, leftovers forgotten,
and puts me down in his bedroom, closing the door. We
kiss as I remove his button down, caressing his chest as I
undo the buttons. We kiss after I throw my t-shirt on the

floor. He unclasps my bra and I hiss as his hand grazes my nipple. My jeans. His. Our underwear—all disappear, and we stand in front of each other naked, with just the light of the streetlights outside permeating through the sheer curtain.

There is no awkwardness, it is two people who know each other, body and heart, stepping toward each other, knowing that tonight is more.

Jon pushes me gently onto the bed and I fall willingly. He lifts my leg and kisses my ankle, and then my calf, my knee... going upper and upper to the apex of my thighs. There are no words as none are needed. He caresses my folds, parting them so he can worship me with his gaze. His tongue touches my sensitive skin and I gasp, but that only makes him more intent to savor me, to coax endless pleasure from each movement of his lips, sucking my clit, as two of his fingers pump into me.

I want him to continue, I want him to stop—I do not know. But *he* knows exactly what he craves. He restarts his journey on my body, kissing my navel, his hands moving along my sides and under my boobs, holding himself over me now, as he takes a nipple in his mouth and sucks the bud until it's hard. And then the other, leaving them sensitive and stiff in the evening air as he moves onto my collarbone, feathering kisses along my skin.

He nibbles at my neck as I can finally touch him as well. My fingers trace the muscles on his back, tender movements reminding me of each dip and peak of him as my foot rubs against his calf.

When his lips get to mine, tasting myself and tasting him with an untamed appetite, his arms box me in. His cock is between my thighs, blessed friction between my mound and his shaft, coating himself in my arousal as we brush against each other.

"I want you inside me," are the words I chose from the thesaurus currently in my heart. "Nothing between us—I am clean, and I am on the shot. I trust you."

"I trust you, too, DJ..."

I don't let him finish but lift my hips so I can get him at my entrance, no doubt in what I want, and as he kisses me like never before, deep and all-consuming, possessive and marking, his dick slides into me. He fills me slowly, one inch at a time, both of us breathing heavily, relishing the indulgence and pleasure.

When he bottoms out, he stills and looks at me with such emotion, that I touch his face in my palms and kiss him lazily. All the feeling in me pours into him with every press of my lips, and every swipe of my tongue against his. Jon starts moving then, his cock in and out of me in a steady deliberate rhythm, delving into my pussy so deep that I gasp with each stroke, basking in bliss.

I am exposed staring back at him as I feel my climax building, tension rising within me. I press my heels against his ass, pulling him even deeper, our bodies move together, the look on his face telling me repeatedly that what we have between us is as inconceivable for him as is for me, and yet just as extraordinary.

I tremble as he kisses me again, and when his thumb presses against my clit, moving in circles, I overload. My senses lost in an exhilarating orgasm, in the indescribable euphoria of a blazing peak I never experienced before. My whole being explodes, no end to the scorching pleasure, as he comes along with me and as I watch him, neck muscles strained, eyes closed, erupting in primal satisfaction, filling me up, his warm cum coating my pussy and changing us.

We fall asleep in each other's arms, Jon collapsed on his back and me at his side, head on his chest holding him tightly, both knowing that we shifted something significant tonight, beyond the 'more', in the wordless tangible reality of us.

DJ

In the morning we attempted to prepare breakfast for Tae, but after the second kitchen fire alarm got set off, we all had cereal. Neither Jon nor I spoke out loud about what transpired yesterday, nor said the words on the tip of our tongues. Yet I know them in my bones, I can feel them each time he looks at me over the island, or in his touch when I pass his coffee cup, and his fingers linger on mine.

I am in love with him. With his kindness and protectiveness. I love his hold and his kiss, and how he makes me laugh. Maybe mostly when he acts as a grunting caveman and mumbles his words as we spar over nothing at the office, causing him to pinch my side and me to mock slap his chest. But then he holds my hand all the way to the car, as I lean on his shoulder.

We take Tabitha to get her things from her house, and it is truly anticlimactic, as Miranda isn't there. With just the maid and cook at home, it takes us less than half an hour to load Jon's Range Rover with what his sister wants to take with her.

Tae seems a bit sad, but I know how to keep her entertained by talking girl stuff. Jon was twitchy in the car on the way there, but he was better toward the end.

When I got kissed like he hasn't seen me in a month and all I could do was hold on to my dear life. Unexpectedly, holding on to his strong arms, feeling my man owning me, is all I could have wanted.

He drops her off at her school and me at my house as he has to go into McAv for the final hangar inspection, and I need to change to meet a real estate agent to look at some office space for my company.

Both my team and I loved staying in the IT department bunker, so I am in two minds on just asking Jon to rent the area from him—though he doesn't need the money, I want to think he enjoys having me around as well. Well, I know some parts of being there are mutually satisfactory to both of us. I smile inwardly.

The minute I get in my house, I realize how little time I have spent here in the past month—it's as if I am in a hotel. I still haven't unpacked everything. All austere and cold, only my home office with papers everywhere and my unmade bed next door.

But there is no smell of burned toast in the air, no Xbox remotes to trip over in the living room. No Greek god reading on his kindle—probably trying to find more big words—on an Adirondack chair with a beer at his side on his deck.

As I shower and change, I keep thinking about the enormity of my feelings for Jon. Feelings I didn't want to admit, with my failed marriage's shadow looming over me. I also know for certain I never loved Richard, not like this. We were just together and then married and then... just there. Catching him with Janine triggered my anger, yes, but the hurt was because of the lying, the cheating. Not because of something fundamental breaking within my heart, no tears or sadness, only hollowness.

When I think of my caveman, I smile without realizing. I miss him at random times and wish he was here now. As he fills my soul every time that dimple shows up and he chuckles from deep within his chest. And seeing him with Tae... makes me think of other futures for us, some I never pictured for myself. Of family dinners and... more.

I hear the doorbell and hurry to the door, but it is too early for my agent. When I spot who it is on my camera, I stop dead right holding the handle, and I think for a second to just leave him hanging. But he wouldn't be here without a reason, and even for a bad reason, I want to know why.

So, I take a deep breath, square my shoulders, and open the door to hear what my ex-husband wants today.

"Well, DJ, long time no see," he grins at me, forgetting we are not best friends. "Aren't you going to invite me in? Maybe offer me a drink?" He grabs my hand but I yank it back, shocked at his gall.

What the actual fuck? There are no better words to be said.

"What the actual fuck, Richard? You are not getting in here and the only drink you are getting from me is in your face. What are you doing here?"

"Ah, I see how it is." He waffles, leaning on my door frame, a foot in the doorway so I can't shut him out. "Well, I think you may want to hear my offer. It's really... too good to pass up."

"Offer?"

"Yep," he continues with a mad look in his eyes, "offer you the chance to give me the full 'Zephyr' software, of course!"

"What the actual fuck—AGAIN. Why would I give you that? You got your half exactly as written in the court order." I am beginning to think the man is going insane, and lucky for me, I can see some dog walkers and people in cars in front of my house.

"That bullshit code you got away with giving me?" he asks, angrier now. "When you realize what damage I can do, you will just give me the 'Zephyr'. I hear you are almost done with it, ready for testing."

"You are here to blackmail me?" I laugh. "With what? You have nothing on me!" I wonder how he knows where I am with the software. When Anya left, I wasn't so close, so how does he know?

"Ah yes, the perfect Dahlia Jara, nothing can touch her!" he mocks waving his hands about, again touching me, picking up a lock of my hair. I bat his hand.

"If your limb gets anywhere near my vicinity again, you lose it!" I warn him, but he just chuckles, putting his hands in his pockets. He came dressed for a date, in an elegant white shirt contrasting his dark hair and eyes, but none of it does anything for me. All I can think of is... yuk.

"Ah baby, you used to love it when I had my hands on you," my ex teases and I cringe, "but regardless, there is something that you have to lose now."

I add nothing, just look at him. He is so confident, to show up at my house, threatening something obscure. I don't know what it can be, and I dread it.

"Nothing to say? That's unusual for you, DJ. You always liked to have the last word. How about you let me in, or the whole block will hear the audio of a very interesting video of your new man?" His words sucker punch me and I look around for neighbors who could be within hearing distance—I didn't expect it to be about Jon, and definitely I never thought Richard would be the one to bring it up.

"If you need more motivation, you can either hear me out, or this recording gets straight to a judge, and trust me, this one is admissible."

The toad of a man got me—I can't afford to let him go without seeing what lies they manufactured now.

"Fine, come in the hallway only. But I am leaving the door open," I say as I wave him in begrudgingly.

"Whatever you need, baby, won't make the end of the conversation any different." He struts in and smiles at me in his asshole way. I sit at the back of the entrance, ready to bolt if he attempts to close the door.

He pulls out his phone and presses play.

The video shows a house party with several folk dancing in the background, and discarded alcohol bottles everywhere. I spot Nathan pouring himself a drink as he yells,

"Yo! We got a wannabe YouTube director here! Man, no need to film Jon getting pissed. It's a common occurrence!"

"Oh, let him be, who gives a fuck what he's recording," I make out Jon's voice and then he appears in the shot, basically granting permission for the video.

I can understand how this will be going bad soon, even from the implications made by Nate that his friend is always drunk.

Jon is stumbling around the room, holding a glass of amber-colored liquid, when he runs into a redhead.

"Hey big man," she purrs, "you want some molly?" and she hands him a questionable pill, and my breath catches for a second, but he pushes her away.

"Nah, too much for me these days. Got this though if you want to go light it up out back." He holds up something which resembles a joint and puts his arm around the woman and they disappear from view.

"Fuck man, you got the girl again? Lucky you—just put that out if you start fucking!" Nathan screams after them, and then the video cuts off.

I am quiet, mind whirling, trying to make sense of what I saw and the horrible interpretations of the recording. Although I didn't see him take anything, and alcohol is not illegal, he is holding a potential joint which—without a medical license—is illegal in Florida. Jon also mentions some historic possible usage of MDMA and Nate is doing him absolutely no favors, blabbering about the women in Jon's past.

If this video comes up in a custody hearing, it will look as if he has substance abuse issues, and combined with the women, it will tank any potential for getting Tae. I am afraid now when I peer at Richard and I can see the triumph on his face.

"Checkmate DJ—so what will it be? 'Zephyr' or Jon's custody of his sister and, of course... his reputation? You choose, but I expect the software by tomorrow. Oh, and don't assume that video you have of Miranda to be usable—Ramsay bought the restaurant and will make sure the source is destroyed, and we will say you fabricated it. You know—smart programmer like yourself, a bit of editing won't be out of reach etc." He crosses his arms and stares me down, smug bastard, and then sashays out of my house, leaving me reeling.

There is only one thing I can do.

JON

I was beyond anxious by the time we got to my former stepmother's in the morning. My knuckles were white from grabbing the steering wheel, and DJ basically had to yank my hand off it to calm me down. Luckily, Tabitha was on her phone, so didn't notice. And even luckier, Miranda wasn't home.

Tae's disappointment was aparent, especially as she texted in advance, so I tried to distract her by discussing school. Dahlia actually succeeded by talking nonstop about TV shows and admiring her clothes and knick-knacks while helping her pack.

By the time we got back to the car, I had to pull my girlfriend to me and kiss her breathlessly, as without her I would have lost it. I almost told her right then and there, on Miranda's driveway, with my sister looking for her headphones upstairs. With the maid spying on us to check if we won't steal the silverware. I should have told her last night, when she put her arms around me. Or when she placed the last egg roll on my plate, as she knows they are my favorite.

And I will tell her tonight. I will put her over my shoulder as she giggles and carry her into my bedroom, sit her on the bed and tell her that she is my rock and that I can't get the smell of her hair out of my mind. That I wasn't looking for anything when I walked into her brothers' shop weeks ago, but I ended up fighting with her over a shirt and falling head over heels for her. That I hope she loves me back.

My day at the office has been quite bland, with some audit meetings running over lunch, then time to review reports on sales before we submit them to the board.

I am ready to meet the Lexingtons for the custody arrangement tomorrow before we go to the judge. My lawyer again is delighted we have so much video evidence and has prepared the paperwork for full guardianship to transfer over to me. I wasn't sure my sister would want to move in with me, but Tae assured me that although she loves her mom, she would rather stay with me and only visit with her every other weekend and on some holidays.

By 3 pm I finish the bulk of my work and think to call DJ to make sure she wants to meet at the house after I get Tae—and realize I am casually planning a school pickup—when my VP walks into my office, with a serious expression on her face.

"Hey Mike, how can I help?" I ask in a good mood.

"Jon, I wanted to invite you to conference room 2. The board is waiting for you there."

"What?" I almost fall off my seat. "Why are they here? We had nothing set up? Who called them?"

"It is probably better if you come see for yourself," she avoids the question and ignores me as she goes towards the meeting, leaving me scrambling after her as a kindergarten kid following the teacher.

As I walk in, I am stunned—the entire board is there, people my father knew and some fresh faces. Ten executives sat down waiting for me like an unruly child coming to get scolded. Ever since I took over from my dad, they have been judgemental assholes trying to second guess every move I made. Only by sheer luck and grit I managed to keep them in check and to hold my job as CEO of McAv as many of them don't approve of me, despite lining their pockets with our profits, with more money than my father ever made.

"Hello everyone, I see I am late for something. Could anyone let me know to what?" I start out strong as these sharks can smell blood in the water and are ready to tear me to pieces if I falter.

Gus Lemkin, one of the 'old guard' members with his white hair, fitted three-piece suit and expensive Rolex, points to a chair at the end of the table, like I am interviewing for X Factor. The hell with that, and I take my normal seat in the center, staring them down.

"Jon, thanks for coming on such short notice," Amelia Ibrahim, one of the newest board members after acquiring a lot of our stock, starts. "Some disturbing news came to our attention, and we wanted to discuss it with you."

Came to their attention? I glance over at Mike, leaning by a wall, no emotion on her face whatsoever but avoiding my gaze.

"OK, so what is it? Financials are good, Inspection passed."

They shuffle in their chairs, at least some of them looking contrite.

"Firstly, can you confirm that we had a data breach? I understand we had a case of corporate espionage," Gus begins the interrogation.

Well, fuck, I had hoped that hadn't reached them.

"We had some documents sent to one of our competitors, yes, but we found the person and she is no longer with the company and we have disabled the means of communication she was using. We are continuing to monitor email traffic and the spot checks on our employees—I am confident that Lex Aviation won't be getting any more of our suppliers, and none jumped ship in the last months or so. Is that it?"

"Thank you for clarifying Jon," he corporate-speaks at me, "but can you confirm if the police arrested the person?"

"Unfortunately, we didn't have any evidence which would stand up in court due to Florida's two side consent rule, so the videos we had couldn't be used. We also cut a deal with her so we can get her files and any proof she had against Miranda, which is obviously more important," I admit, tapping my fingers against the table.

"But aren't all employees asked to sign a waiver to that law? We must have had cameras on her?" he presses on, clearly on a witch hunt.

"Anya has confirmed she made both me and Michaela sign exceptions for her. Mike can confirm as well."

"I can't support that actually, I would've never signed anything like that," she pipes up and the rug is being pulled from under me. Mike said that? Fuck, is it she who called the Board?

"What do you mean, you were there when we caught her? She specifically mentioned she made us both sign!"

"I do not recall having signed anything Jon, I am sorry. If you check the files, it is only a form you endorsed, which is in the folders." I am stunned—one of the people I relied on the most in the world just threw me to the sharks. If the board wasn't in the room, I would start screaming at her.

"Apologize for interrupting," Amelia intervenes, "but did you say 'Anya', your executive assistant?"

I do not answer, but I see the mood shift even more, everyone looking extremely shocked, exchanging glances.

"That is worrying news Jon, especially as you hired her personally, direct interview and all that." Gus is going through some papers on his desk, and it dawns on me the size of the setup I walked right in. They know who the leak was and are ready to crucify me for it. Still, Mike won't look me in the eye. I won't bother pointing out it was my VP who brought Anya in for the interview.

"Well, I admit it was a bit of a whirlwind, but let's all take a breath and consider we caught the person. The company is secure. I just sat with all our suppliers, and everyone is happy if not happier with us now." I try to get them back to reality.

"Right, the company is secure," Gus mumbles, and I know this is more than a witch hunt. It is a goddamn execution, and they have more they want to say.

"Jon, you not only hired the EA, but recently you also got an IT firm to work with us, 'J-AvTech'," the new board member comments, "owned by Dahlia Jara."

Where are they going with this?

"I have indeed—the weather predictor will be one of our biggest draws for our planes—you all know those rich people like nothing more than saving money and owning a unique piece of kit." I move in my seat, surveying the room. Some of them listen to me, but many watch Gus and, even worse, some of my father's previous friends, including Lemkin, follow my VP, making me clench my fists. "Is there a question in there?"

"Yes, actually. We got this 'personal relationship at work' form as well, with your name on it—and hers. A tad worried you are giving your girlfriend millions of dollars. You can see how it looks, Jon," Gus says.

"Are you fucking kidding me?" I explode. "She wasn't my girlfriend then. Also, she created Hove. It's not like she's a stripper, but is recognized in the industry, and we are lucky to have her. We only wrote the form to be out in the open. Otherwise, I suspect you'd all be chastising me for not reporting it!"

"She is well known indeed, but so is her husband, right? We saw he works for Lexington. The competition, you admit, has been spying on us. I thought they just presented a similar software?" the old boy presses on.

"Ex-husband. Actually, it was Dahlia who found out how the data was being transmitted, and she absolutely hates him for trying to pass her code as hers. She's here to make sure he and Miranda are taken down a peg or two."

"Quite a complicated story you weave, Jon, but we are beginning to think it is you who is out of the loop." Ms. Ibrahim looks a bit disappointed in me now and starts picking at the papers on the table. "For example, you say Dahlia Jara hates her husband, but then, why was he at her house this morning?"

What? This morning? I just dropped her off. She was supposed to meet her real estate agent.

Amelia picks up a few printed images and walks over to my chair. The click clack of her heels is foreboding, and I don't even acknowledge what she is wearing as she stops next to me, pulling her a strand of her curly black hair behind her ear. She lays the first photos in front of me and I freeze.

Richard is standing at DJ's door, leaning in as if he owns the place.

She puts another picture down. This time, he is touching her. He is fucking touching her! I grab the paper to look in detail. His fucking hand is on my woman! I am about to get out of my chair when she adds two more.

First—he is in the house! She let him inside her home?

Second—he is touching her hair!

I am seething, wanting to squash the images and wipe them from my brain. But after the reporter and Miranda,

I hope there is more to the pictures. DJ would not do this to me. She would never.

"As you can see, they don't appear to be at war with each other, more like the opposite," Gus—the son of a bitch—talks.

"These pics show nothing. Even exes talk to each other from time to time."

"If you say so." Mike is the one who starts moving around the room now, hands behind her back, like she is Picard on the deck of the Starship Enterprise. "But then, if your girlfriend isn't working with Richard, why would she have come to the office two hours ago and taken every piece of code off our network? Here—we have her on camera. Explain this."

She presses a remote she had in her hand and the TV in the room shows a video from the IT department. It's a bit dark, but we can make out DJ getting to her computer with what I assume is an external hard drive, and plug that in. She clicks on her keyboard a few times, then starts pacing, chewing on her nails as she monitors the screens on her desk. She is as beautiful as ever, but I can see she is stressed, watching the screen every few seconds, and putting her hands in her hair.

My VP fast forwards on the video, and my brunette goes back to her desk, unplugging the hard drive. Her shoulders sag as she casts another glance around the office, looking defeated, then walking out.

I do not know how to react. I can't believe she would have done that. This morning I would have never thought she would have her ex anywhere near her. The code... she took the code? Why did she come into work? She had it all on the cloud. I didn't understand, and I needed to get out of this room to see her, call her, and make her explain.

"We realize this is troubling you," Mike continues. "But you can understand why the board is here. First the slip-ups, missing meetings, losing suppliers, me having to step into critical sessions. Hiring an EA who spies on us behind your back with your permission so we can't prosecute her. We are in a partnership with your girlfriend with a damaging contract for us, where she owns the software, just uses our airplanes to test it out. Now it appears she not only lied to you, but ran away with all the work."

I have no answer, knowing exactly what comes next.

"Jon, the Board has looked over the evidence, and we think it is probably better if you take a little sabbatical until this all clears over." Lemkin twists the knife in my back, as I struggle to breathe still staring at the pictures in front of me and the video paused of DJ running away.

"Michaela has volunteered to pick up your duties," another suit says, but I stop listening. I get out of my chair and walk out.

As I exit the room, I turn back and my heart breaks looking at Mike. But she doesn't look at all upset. The smile on her face makes my skin crawl, and I know I have been played. She has been playing me for fifteen years and has now finally got me where she wanted me. She wanted the company, and now, despite years of profits and successes, because of some of my blunders and DJ, she has it.

But McAv needs to wait, as I have to find Dahlia and have her explain. I need her to make it better, as my mind can't comprehend what I just saw, and I hope I can get to her and that everything will be OK.

I am out in the corridor and stumble with my phone, dialing her number.

It rings and rings and rings. Then voicemail.

Fuck!

I call her again. And voicemail again.

I check my texts and I notice one from her.

Don't wait up, I have something I need to do urgently. I'll see you tomorrow before the custody meeting.

What does that mean? Where did she go?

I reply, typing with trembling fingers. *DJ, call me asap... What the fuck is going on? Did you take the code? Why was Richard at your house?*

There are a couple of missed calls from Nate also, but returning them is the last thing on my mind.

I get to my office and just grasp at my phone, hoping the woman I am in love with gets back to me and that it's not all an absolute disaster.

DJ

The airplane wheels hit the tarmac and I jolt awake. I can't believe I fell asleep, but I was absolutely worn after having to run into McAv. I dashed in there immediately after Richard left and cleared any bits of code in their local drives, as I suspect some of my teams have saved locally from time to time. I know I did, as even I got a bit careless some days. No way was I leaving anything there if someone was still feeding information to Lex Aviation, as they must be if they knew how close I was.

I check my phone as I get in the back of my Uber, and I see 10 missed calls and several voicemails from Jon.

"Shit!" I read the text from him—how the hell did he hear about that? I press the green icon and he answers immediately.

"DJ! What the fuck? I have been calling for hours!" He sounds agitated. I can imagine him pacing around his office, and I am beginning to think something is horribly wrong.

"Sorry Jon, I was on a plane, and I fell asleep. How did you know about my ex at my house?"

"Plane? Where did you go? Shit! Did you run? Fuck—they were right, weren't they? You took the code and ran!"

"What? Who is 'they'? I don't have a response to that—I had to get to Colorado fast, that's why I had to fly here. Can you slow down a bit? Are you OK? I am worried now."

"Am I OK? No, I am not OK—my girlfriend has apparently been collaborating with her ex-husband, took her code for which we had a contract and ran out of state! All that and the board just booted me out of my job between Anya and you!"

"What? They did what? Hell! I haven't been 'collaborating' with anyone and I did not take the software. I just cleared the local drives as there is still someone giving them information! I will be back tomorrow, but can you please stop accusing me without talking to me!" I yell over the phone.

"I would have talked to you if you would have answered your fucking phone!" he yells back. "What do you want me to think—they had pictures of him at your house! He was touching you! And now you are all the way across the country?"

"Jon, calm down. I can't talk to you while you're like this." I take a breath. "Look, I am sorry about your job, but I think it's all related. I need to get something from here, then I will be right back. Please, trust me on this. Nothing is going on between Richard and me, it's the same as with the reporter and whatever other shit they have been trying to pull, twisting everything. My driver is just pulling in now. I am taking the plane back at midnight. I will be home by 6 am. Just... just hold on, OK, caveman?" I ask softly at the end.

"I... I don't know Avril," he whispers into the phone. "I don't know anymore, and I can't talk to you like this when you are miles away."

He cuts the call abruptly, and it comes off as getting punched in the gut, his last words so low, the hurt in his voice traveling through the air and hitting me straight on. I wipe tears from my eyes as I get out of the car and shoot a text to my sister.

Luckily, Nathan waits for me outside his house and notices me being upset.

"Hey warrior princess, long time no see. Come in, let's find you those tapes, huh? Are you OK? Have you have been crying? How is our boy? Left him a couple of voice-mails, but I haven't heard back from him."

"Man," I correct automatically and smile, remembering our first conversation. "He doesn't like to be called a boy."

"Ha, well, speak for yourself. I am two months older than him, so I can call him whatever I want. So, what's up? You got lucky I was in Vegas and could get here so fast—if I were in Monaco or the Philippines..."

"I don't know the whole thing, Nate, but as I said on the phone, Tae's custody arrangement may depend on what we see on the videos. It doesn't look good if they just show what they tried to blackmail me with. Please try Jon again," I ask as I sit down on his sofa, take my jacket off and sigh, leaning against the cushions. "We didn't end our call just now on the best of terms. I am under the impression that they are trying to manipulate him, and I am not there to explain."

"Uh, will do, princess. I've put the box of all the old hard drives in my office, you can go check it out in a minute, but first let me get you a drink. Not to sound insensitive but... you look like shit."

He grins at me, then brings me a cup of coffee, which I warm my hands against.

"Thanks, Nathan, I truly appreciate all of this—coming all the way to meet me at your holiday home, the coffee, all of it—not the 'you look like shit' bit. When I called you earlier today after seeing the video, I had hoped you knew something to clarify exactly has happened, but I am even more impressed you had the videos."

"Yeah, I keep them for a long time, you never know! Is Jon not having the best of days, eh?"

"I am genuinely worried about him. They kicked him out of his job and tried to make it like I have cheated on him and stolen the software we had."

"They did what? Fucking hell—Mike didn't stop them?"

"I don't know, he didn't say. Maybe I need to call him back," I wonder, feeling more and more anxious about the whole thing.

"Do you want to look through the tapes first? By the way, princess—the man is gone for you; you know that right?"

"I hope so, I am definitely gone for him," I confess, needing to say that out loud to someone. "When I return to Kerrington, I'll show him that I am not what they make me out to be."

"Umm... he does know why you are here, right? You didn't just tell him you're in Colorado and left it at that? Can't blame a guy for being a tad upset if his girlfriend just goes away with not so much of an explanation the day he gets fired, right?" Nate's blue eyes are piercing me with concern.

Oh.

"Oh—I am an idiot! I was just trying to fix things..."

"Yeah, 'oh'! Gosh, how did you two find each other? A spilled coffee meet-cute? You are both idiots! Him for not recognizing what he had immediately, and you for taking him for granted."

"Umm, technically there was a coffee spill involved," I admit, and Nate mumbles, "Of course there was," with his slight Irish accent. "But you are right, I should have explained better what is going on. It's just that on the phone earlier, I was shocked to hear about the whole thing, and I didn't find my words."

I pick up my smartphone to call him, but he doesn't respond. Shit!

I try again and still nothing, so all I can do is send him a message and hope it's enough, obviously not including a reference to drugs in a text string.

I am at Nathan's in Aspen. Richard was at my house trying to blackmail me with an old video of yours, so I am here to find some recordings from back then. I will tell you all about it tomorrow. Please wait for me.

I almost write 'I love you' at the end but stop myself. I want to tell him that when I am in his arms, encompassed by his manly smell and running my hands through his hair looking him in the eyes, not in a 'whatsup' text.

"Come on, best friend, time to go do some digging." I put the coffee mug down with fake confidence. "Let's see these videos and save our boy."

JON

I had to shut the phone call with DJ down before either of us said something we would regret. It's all too much. I was already home when she managed to get back to me, the whole day—unreal from the excellent start, to getting Tabitha sorted, to the disaster of the afternoon.

My driver picked up my sister as I was in no shape to drive, and she is upstairs now doing her homework, and I was on my second beer sitting on my chair, feeling totally lost. I have no job. My girlfriend is, apparently, with my oldest friend and there is extortion going on. And Mike stabbed me in the back.

I just don't know what to do. All I can see is that picture of his hand on her hair, and I want to go punch him in the face. And I am so mad at her for gallivanting off without finding me and telling me what is happening.

The doorbell rings and as I look through the glass pane in the door, my heart flutters as there is a brunette standing there and, for a millisecond, I think it's DJ. But I deflate when I realize this woman is taller, and the red streaks in her shoulder length hair give her away.

"Laura, what are you doing here? Can I help you with anything? Your sister is not here," I ask as I open the door for her. She gives me a once over and shakes her head, then struts right in.

"I know. She texted me to come over to make sure if you are OK, you big lug! Here!" She plants a plastic box in my hands and says, "Bought dinner as instructed. I hear you are just as hopeless in the kitchen as lil D, which I would have thought impossible. She only had the firefighters called two times on her—though the second time she may have done it on purpose to hit on one of them."

DJ sent her sister to bring me food? Firefighters?

"By the confused face you are displaying, I suspect she said nothing about it, huh?" she continues as she helps herself to a beer from my fridge, puts her cane on the side and sits down on a chair by the island. I am a tad stunned how I just *grew* a Jara sister in my kitchen.

"No, she didn't. I got a text saying she's in Colorado and then we had a phone call fight. She then sent another text which—frankly made me even more upset," I admit, taking another beer for myself and sitting across from Laura, hoping she can shed some light on whatever is happening.

"Ah, what you got is my *hermanita* in 'fixer' mode, basically—welcome to the family!" she grins. "DJ does not ask for permission, nor take any advice before she is off to fight her battles. Saving maidens, killing dragons, investigating whatever she's off now with... she just goes and does it for the people she cares for. Has been doing it since we were little—my mum was mad with her running off to save the cat-of-the-day and not telling anyone. Once she went to our brother's preschool to punch a kid in the nose for bullying Marcus. She was nine, we had to call the police as she just walked all the way there from her own classes by herself and her teachers—rightfully panicked."

Saving maidens? Shit—that's what she did with Tae—just dropped everything and ran after her. Same with the fax!

"Ah, I see you now realize you have experienced this before. It's just who she is... she sees a wrong, she is going to right it. I hope you can hack it, big man." Laura eyes me with interest.

"I..." I struggle to find my words, "thank you for telling me all this. I have seen her do that before, I just didn't associate it."

"Don't sweat it, Jon. My sister without a map is really like one of her video games on 'hard mode'. You are doing pretty good, you know—she doesn't pick up that sword out for just anyone—well, unless it's animals and children, of course."

"You think?" All the insecurities revealed in the past day come to life.

"Oh dear, you are lucky she thinks you're pretty," she mocks as she rolls her eyes at me. "Dahlia sent me with food over for you and your sister. She is basically living here with YOU or working with YOU. Where is she tonight? On the other side of the country trying to help YOU. Congrats again, big lug, don't fuck it up!" She polishes her beer in record time, as I can only look at the patterns of marble on my island countertop.

"Laura," I start unsure how to continue without digging myself in with the sister, but after the pictures, I have to ask. "Do you think DJ will ever want to get back together with Richard? They were married, after all."

"HAHAHA" the brunette bursts into laughter and I have to shush her to not get Tabitha interested. "That is funny, Jon, I have to say! 'Not in a million years' is the answer. They were never right for each other and without the accidental wedding, they would have broken things off a long time ago. And after the Janine incident... no way! What is triggering this burst of concern?"

"I got shown some pictures with him at her house earlier today. DJ says he was there to blackmail her."

"Richard? At DJ's house? Trust me, big man, she wouldn't have let him in unless she had no choice. He definitely had something on her to allow him anywhere near her person. Have a little faith, she hasn't stopped thinking about your Thor-like ass ever since the shop 'event'," she winks at me.

"Now—one thing we ask in the Jara household is... are we drinking or are we... *Drinking*? You look like you could use the second version tonight. My son is at my brother's, and I have nothing better to do than babysit you; so, come on, bring two more beers over and I will tell you what DJ's weakness really is." Laura smiles at me and despite her poking at me, I appreciate her being here a lot. Her walking me off a ledge when it comes to the ex.

"OK Ms. Laura, let's *Drink*! I think I know what her weakness is already, by the way. Starts with a 'c'."

"Yeah, yeah. Not talking about your penis just yet, maybe next time." She snickers at me, and the weight lifts off my shoulders a bit, with a friend to joke with me and a couple of cold ones.

"We know it's not THAT—well, hopefully not just THAT," I laugh back and sit down. "And we both know it's cronuts!" I get confirmation that I answered correctly with another nod of approval from a Jara sibling, as we start the *Drinking*.

***

My head is pounding, and my mouth is dry as I roll my blanket over my shoulders, trying to settle on the relatively uncomfortable couch I had the honor of sleeping on. After the alcoholic coma I almost got in while struggling to match Laura's penchant for spirits, I told her to take the main bedroom as I wanted to wait for DJ anyway. I was in no shape to climb the stairs, but I was not going to admit to that.

I get up to drink some water and rinse my teeth with mouthwash in the downstairs bathroom before I hear the key turning in the front door and I jump up. But this time I exhale freely as it is my warrior, back from whatever quest she was on.

Stopping two feet from her, I say nothing—she looks tired, her hair a mess, dressed in loose jeans and a black shirt with an old leather jacket. Yet she is still beautiful as ever to me, grasping my spare key from under the pot outside. When she glances at me with red-rimmed eyes, the

239

worry in them makes me move and put my arms around her, holding my woman with no words.

She hugs me back and burrows her face in my chest, breathing against my t-shirt and as easy as that, all is right in the world.

"Hey Avril," I say against her hair, inhaling her scent.

"Hey caveman," she answers softly, then pulls back a bit, looking at me with those eyes of hers which melt me. My heart goes 'thump' as well at the sound of our names for each other. "Messed up yesterday. I am sorry for going without talking to you. I was a bit of an idiot." She smiles shyly, and it's a side of her I don't see often, and I am grateful she can be vulnerable with me. That I get to prop her up when she needs me to, remembering that night in the car, after the reporter, when she needed to hold my hand to calm down.

"You were a bit of an idiot. But I also didn't help matters by having a freak out over the phone. But as you did send your sister with food, I might forgive you." I put my hands around her face and kiss her forehead, and the sigh of relief from her is all I needed to hear. She is home, and she is mine.

"Come on, let's sit and you can tell me exactly what happened yesterday." I pull her down on the sofa and arrange her legs over my thighs.

"Where do I even start?" she begins, but then looks at my pillow and blanket. "Why are you sleeping down here?"

"Well, if you must know, your sister basically drank me under the table. So, I sent her up to the bedroom."

"Couldn't get up the stairs?" she guesses correctly but I refuse to confirm or deny. "That will teach you. Laura used to work in bars. She can out-drink us all!"

"I can see that as more of a challenge for the future," I comment, and the grin on DJ's face is blinding.

"Future?" The grin transforms into her charming shy smile and all I can do is pull her in for a proper kiss. She seems to agree as she responds eagerly, gripping my arms and climbing in my lap.

"Yep, future. I said I will not let you go, and I meant it. But I may need to punch that ex-husband of yours soon, though," I commit and her face lights up once more.

"You will have to get behind me on that! But first you must believe that I wasn't cheating with him, I don't know what pictures they showed you—also, who is 'they'?—, he came to blackmail me with a video of you from a party about four years back. He weaselled his way inside after threatening to have the neighbors hear it, but that's pretty much it. Oh, and he kept trying to touch me—the snake—and I kept having to bat his hand away. After our call, I checked my outside cameras and spotted a guy in a car recording the whole thing."

"Shit—it means he was more prepared than we gave him credit for. He probably knew what he was doing, and they cut that film to exact times so they can just show me snips when it suited them!" I am mad now for being so gullible and even thinking that there was something there.

"Hey, don't beat yourself up." My girlfriend holds me tighter. "If they would have brought up pictures of you and an ex taken at your house from the same day we had a really sexy make-out session on a driveway, I wouldn't have reacted very well myself. Speaking of..."

DJ gets up and goes to collect her bag. I didn't even notice she dropped by the entrance. She pulls out her laptop, sitting back down next to me and starts to pull some folders up.

"I copied all these from Nathan's hard drives he had at his house in Aspen. You are very lucky your friend keeps all his security tapes for five years."

"Yeah, after he had a break in a while back, he holds on to everything—is that where this party was? At Nate's? Four years ago? I think I remember bits of it. I was pretty much out of it."

"It was exactly the point Richard was trying to make. He had a video of you not-so-charmingly drunk, and with Nathan complimenting your... lady catching skills."

"Umm," is the only answer that I could come up with.

"Settle down, I am aware you had girlfriends before me. You know that doesn't faze me, more like I appreciate the experience you bring to the table." She winks at me, and I shake my head at her making a joke when talking about this. "The problem is the recording also had you taking out something which resembled a joint, and saying something along the lines of you don't do harder drugs 'anymore'. I can't remember the exact phrase and he didn't send me the file, unfortunately."

"What? I don't recall any of that. You must know, I haven't taken anything in years! Fuck, this is messed up! If they show that video at the meeting with the Lexingtons, they can bury me, and I'll never see Tabitha again."

"I know Jon, that's why I called Nathan immediately after Richard left and asked him if he had any memories of the day and if he had any security footage of the party to see for myself exactly what happened. Then I went to the office and deleted all my software there—that's what the blackmail was for, by the way—and got straight to the airport after that."

"Did you find anything?"

"Well, I found something, two videos actually... There are only outside cameras at your friend's house, so I can't confirm if it's the same person who recorded you, however-er."

She puts on the first video.

It's me and a girl, walking in Nate's backyard and then sitting down on a bench by a fire pit, but still close enough to the dwelling so that the image is pretty clear. She lights up a cigarette shaped object and offers it to me, but I shake my head at her, take the bud from her and throw it in the flames, then get up on shaky legs, drag her over and give her a sloppy kiss, almost falling over. The images then show me leading her back inside.

"It gets even better. This is from earlier in the night," my girlfriend puts on the second one.

I am outside on the front porch, sitting on the swing, holding a bottle of what I assume is whiskey, taking a swig and staring at the snow-covered hills around me. A blond guy comes over and shakes my hand, saying some muffled words to me, and then he pulls out something and offers it to me.

DJ increases the volume.

"Here you go Jon, you want to smoke a bit with me? When in Rome and all that..." he asks.

"Nah dude, I don't do any of that shit anymore. Ever since my sister was born, I swore I'll do good by her and stop with the dope, setting a positive example for her."

"Ah, chill man, it's not actually marijuana, it's just a regular cig I rolled—saving money and all that!" He offers it to me again and I accept it but put it in my back pocket.

"Thanks, maybe I'll smoke it later," I say and return to my bottle.

"The video goes on a bit, with you drinking almost half the whiskey and then going inside. The guy leaves after a few minutes as you just admire the landscape and ignore him altogether," she fills me in. "So, at least we can counter it all by showing you didn't actually do any drugs, and that the joint may not even have been a 'joint' in the first place. The 'being an example for your sister'... that... that is pretty sweet, caveman," she beams and makes me so happy seeing her joy.

"WOW!" I exclaim. "That is amazing! Shit—that was very close!" I get off the couch and start pacing the room, hands on my hips, taking deep breaths, awestruck that we have evidence now to counter the blackmail and get me Tae.

"Indeed it was," she agrees and gets up after me, stopping me and taking my hand. "Good thing you are a really great guy—even halfway through a bottle."

"I am, huh? A great guy?" I pull her close to me again, rejoicing in the feel of her body, wishing my house wasn't full of various sisters so I can get DJ's clothes off right here.

"Someone is fishing for compliments," she comments, giggling.

"Mmm, more like take what I'm given." I nibble at her neck, tasting her sweet skin.

"By the way, do you know who that guy is?" DJ switches subjects and I nod. As yes, I recognize who he is, and only cements the betrayal I felt yesterday.

"I do, and I have an idea of exactly how to use all that. But that's for later. It's half-past six in the morning, and right now, I want to hold my woman, have a shower with her, have something to eat—yes, maybe her. Then we can go kick some ass."

I sway her in my embrace for a bit, and we start dancing slowly with no music in my living room, reveling in the quiet and in us. The warmth of her perfect curves glued on me, her hair caressing my tattoos, an excellent start of the day if I ever had one.

"Jon, I want to say something."

"Hmm," I mumble, just enjoying moving with her, dumbfounded how it was all so close to the edge yesterday and now I have my lady in my arms, and confidence we can fix it all together. And that I too have something to tell her.

"Jon..." she starts again and this time she puts her palms on my face, the feel of her soft skin against my beard making me smile, thinking of other soft areas my beard will touch.

"Yes?"

"I want to say... I know it seems insane, and that we have only known each other for like a month—and we have stupid fights. Your former stepmother and my ex are crazy. And it's all up in the air with your job and I probably shouldn't say anything now, and if it's all too much, you need to tell me. And... but... I want to say it now, Jon... I... I." She is absolutely adorable as she is unraveling in front of me, blushing like I've never seen her, and I can only stop her with what I have been wanting to express myself.

"Shh, stop rambling, Avril, it's my turn. Look at me." She listens for a change. "I love you, Dahlia Jara."

"What? I was supposed to tell you I love you!" She seems panicked by my interruption, but then her eyes grow bigger realizing what I just confessed. "Oh!"

"Come here, DJ." My lips capture hers hungrily and I am overwhelmed by the sensation of kissing the woman I love and who loves me back, by the staggering feelings revealed between us.

She moans against me, and I want to lift her and have her against the wall. Only our guests upstairs prevent me from doing just that. So, I settle on grabbing her ass and continue to dive into her mouth, owning all of her, as she owns all of me, digging her hands him my hair, pulling her to me.

"Eww get a room, you two!" I hear Laura's voice as she is coming down the stairs, breaking us up. "Or, seeing as I had your room, at least wait until I leave. I don't need nightmares. Hey sis, I see you got your man back—took good care of him in your absence, but the lad can't hold his liquor. *Tío* Antonio will have a field day at Christmas! Tell me there's coffee," she has a little monologue with herself and goes to the kitchen looking for her brew. "Oh, and Jon, your sister relayed not to wake her before 8 or she will kill you."

"I doubt this is what you imagined if you ever thought of having three ladies in the house," DJ says, still in my arms, shaking her head at her sibling's 'I don't give a shit' attitude.

"I don't think I ever imagined all this, but I wouldn't change this for anything," I declare as I give her another squeeze, then get her hand and take us to get coffees as well, as a plan on tackling our enemies formulates in my head.

"We need to go talk to my former EA first," I start telling DJ my intentions as I watch Laura putting more milk in her coffee than actual coffee, then taking it outside on the terrace.

"Huh? What does Anya have anything to do with this now?" my girlfriend asks, confused.

"We asked her to give us what she had on Miranda. But I don't believe Miranda was actually her contact."

"Who is it then? Richard?"

"I will tell you on the drive there. But first, finish your drink, and then I am dragging you in the shower. I need my breakfast," I grin at her, knowing exactly what I will be feasting on.

DJ

The drive to Anya's followed a chaotic breakfast with Jon slightly lost between three women chattering. He mustered through it as he kept his hand on my lower back or held me at his side, grounding himself. Well, after his private first breakfast in the shower.

My sister volunteered to take Tabitha to school, so we went straight to his ex-assistant's flat, and en route he told me all that happened with Michaela. How she threw him under the bus and lied to the board about the forms. He also thinks she is working with Miranda and Richard and is counting that this trip to Anya's will give us more evidence.

As we arrive in an unsavory part of town, the block of flats looks like it's seen better days, and the street is lined with boarded businesses and homeless people squatting.

"Umm, are you sure she lives here?" I ask as I thought McAv paid quite well.

"That's what we have in the personal details from her at work. Come on, let's go in. She didn't answer her phone, but maybe she's home."

"OK let's try but I hope you still have rims on your car when we return," hinting at some local boys currently eyeing his flashy SUV.

He is about to go talk to them when someone yells from above.

"Hey Jimmy! Tim! Stop scaring the tourists! That dude will give you $100 if his ride is still intact when he gets back!" A woman's voice makes the lads shrug and Jon nods at them, confirming the future 'transaction'.

When I look up, I just see a flurry of blond hair.

"I guess you were right. She's home," I say.

"Yes, and she also wants to talk to us based on the parlay opportunity we just got," my boyfriend concludes correctly.

After climbing the five stories, I am huffing a bit, but Jon—the fucker—is fit as a fiddle and volunteers some unwanted advice.

"Well, DJ, maybe you need to reconsider coming on that run with me next time." He grins.

"Maybe I will. Or maybe I'll just put jelly in your sneakers and set some ants on you."

"Oh, Avril, touched a sore point, have I?"

"I'll give you a sore point in a moment," I pant. "Right after I catch my breath."

"Are you two done? I don't have all day to watch your nauseating banter." Anya sits at her front door, dressed in an oversized t-shirt and yoga pants, but unlike the office she isn't wearing her glasses and her hair is loose, curls everywhere. I think her eyes are a different color also, a bright aqua versus the black I remember. If I didn't recognize the sarcasm in her tone, I wouldn't even have known it was her!

"Anya?" My man is obviously in the same situation. "Umm, thanks for seeing us. May we come in?"

"You may, but I doubt you... can," she answers and as we look into her apartment, we realize why she said that.

The flat is more precisely a single room, with a couch on one side and a desk with some boxes underneath on the other. There is a tiny kitchen in a corner and a door to what I assume is an equally minuscule bathroom in another. I can only presume all her clothes are under the bed, as there doesn't seem to be anywhere else to put anything.

"You—live here? What the hell? I thought McAv gave you a good salary!" Jon is livid as a cockroach passes by in the hallway.

"You did. I just have bigger expenses than that, so this is it," she gives no further information. "So, what do you want?"

"Well, last time we saw each other, we asked you for anything you have on Miranda. Now we realize we may have been misled by other people in my company, and I suspect you know who."

"Hmph, so you finally figured out who the snake in your garden really was, I see. It's always the nice old lady, right?" Anya confirms she knew exactly who it was, validating our assumptions. "Who do you think came up with the idea of the fax? It's a bit before my time. I am surprised you guys put two and two together on that."

"Give us some credit," I intervene. "We aren't total idiots. Just apparently, very trustful."

"I suppose that is true," she ponders. "So, you want dirt on Mrs. Jones today... what's in it for me?"

"What's in it for you? How about giving a bit back after I gave you a really good job and then you stole from me?"

She narrows her eyes at Jon's tirade and looks down for a second before answering with contempt.

"Yeah, the job was good, and you were a decent boss. But you forget I didn't steal for myself. It was your 'friends' who forced me to do it. I did try to help you where I could."

"What? What is that supposed to mean?"

"My role was to mess up your calendar, to 'forget' to send you to meetings and all that. And of course, faxing important documents as you found out. But nobody made me pull the interview with Dahlia a day forward."

"Shit, it was on a Tuesday, I remembered correctly!" he exclaims. "Why would you do that, and how did that help us?"

"Unfortunately, it didn't, as you missed her coming in the morning entirely, and Mike intercepted her. But I knew about the press conference. I overheard Mike on the phone with someone—probably Miranda or your ex-husband—planning it all for Tuesday. So, when you showed up Monday, your VP made me call Lex Aviation and get them to do the announcement right on the spot."

"Sorry, back up a little," I halt her explanation. "Why would they want to have a press conference exactly when our meeting was?"

"Shit!" Jon's loud outburst jolts me as well. "Mike always planned on having us join against Miranda and Richard. We played into it with our little fight! Also, by them announcing it, you would look desperate if we were to talk about it as well." He runs his fingers through his hair as he paces the hallway. "Anya, I don't get it. Why would you try to help? Come to think of it, you never answered DJ's question in the office a while back—why did you get involved in the first place?"

"I tried to help as I couldn't live with myself doing all I was doing, trying to sabotage you, selling secrets," the young woman answers in a sad whisper, and we look at each other, knowing she is telling the truth. "As for why I did it, let's just say they had something on me, and I needed their influence. Maybe one day I will be able to tell you exactly why and how I got involved." Her voice breaks down toward the end, clearly distressed.

I get closer to her and take her hand in mine. She is reluctant at first but then squeezes me right back after a minute.

"Are you OK now? Do you need help?" I ask, looking at her light eyes filled with what I can now see isn't sarcasm, it's despair.

"Yeah, thank you for asking. I got some of my own evidence to protect myself—I can't give you that, though."

"That's fine Anya." Jon also comes closer to us and speaks softly to her, "We will take anything you can share, as we are well aware of how they twist and manipulate. If you need whatever you have for yourself, we understand."

"No, I have something I can share." She goes back into her room and returns with a flash drive. "Here are some emails I forwarded to myself from Michaela's computer. There is an email chain between her and a random email address, so it doesn't look suspicious in a server search, but they forget not to use names in the emails. I have some others which don't impact you, but you can have these."

I pick up the USB from her and take her other hand in mine.

"Thank you, Anya, we genuinely appreciate it. If you need any help, please let us know."

"Thanks Dahlia, but I got it now. You two better get going. The boys downstairs are eager for their payday. And Jon, don't forget to study the other folders I sent you last time. They can really assist you in the long run."

"Will have a look. Thank you as well. If this is as helpful as you say, you may have gotten my company back."

"Good luck," she wishes us as she closes the door.

"Well, that was unexpected," I note as we climb down the stairs.

"Indeed it was. I didn't think we would end up feeling sorry for her," my man admits. "Now, let me see if I actually have $100 cash or if we are about to get my tires slashed." He laughs as we get to the car, hand in hand.

We head on home after finding the money between the two of us, which pleases the lads, as we have to prepare for the meeting tonight with the lawyers and the Lexingtons. With some extra guests, as per Jon's plan.

JON

My palms are sweating, and I feel a chill down my spine as I pace around the event hall we rented for meeting our guests and enemies. It is a round room with several entrances and exits, and ideal for what we planned, with a table in the middle and a skylight above.

DJ looks at me from her laptop and tries to pacify me, as she always does when I am spiraling. She is wearing a simple fitted black dress and I am matching color, fashion not the top of our priorities today. But she still catches my eye every time.

"Caveman, do you want to sit down? Miranda and Ramsay aren't due for a few more minutes. And your lawyer is staring at you funny. Hey Ephraim!" She nods at my attorney who, like her, was working on his computer but lifts his head towards me. His graying hair is cut short and the wrinkles on his face deepen as he scowls at me.

I suppose I should be calm and composed, but I can't stop myself from worrying, despite all the preparations we did, and all the evidence we gathered.

A phone vibrates next to us, and it's showtime.

"I'll go into the other room and intercept him when he arrives." Dahlia gives me a kiss and smacks my ass on the way out, giving me a cheeky wink.

"Ready, Eph?" I ask, but it's more for myself.

"Ready as can be—are you sure you are, though?"

"More than ready. This is long overdue," I confirm just as the main doors open. The Lexingtons and their lawyer, a middle-aged woman in a dark suit I know is called Helena Pruitt, walk in.

Ramsay and the attorney at least have the manners to come shake our hands, as my former stepmother just sits her Chanel-clad bony ass at the table, like she awaits to be served. The elder billionaire with a shaved head and gray eyes is wearing a white t-shirt and brown slacks, as if he came from a round of golf.

"OK, so we are all here. Let's begin the custody discussions," Ephraim begins.

"There will be no need for any 'discussions'," Miranda grins. "Jon knows by now there will be no change to our current set-up, don't you, Jon? Not with the mountains of evidence showing your drug use."

Her lawyer tries to shush her, but she just puts her palms on the table and switches her legs around. A fake Sharon Stone giving us all a cringe sight, luckily hidden. I have to push all my anxiety aside and choose to be in control.

"What evidence would that be?" I assume a relaxed pose myself, arms open, surrounding the chairs next to me. "You are not by any chance mentioning a certain video of me holding something in Aspen a few years back... You do know marijuana has been legal in Colorado since 2012, right?"

"Ha—you admit it!" she pounces. "It's not about the legalities, it's about having my daughter around a known drug user! Probably it's best to show everyone here, so there's no doubt!" She pulls out a tablet and starts playing the video. Everybody watches it with great interest, but I watch just her, staring at her and not the footage, which causes her to falter from her confident stance.

"Not sure what is there to admit. I just stated some facts about the laws in that state," I say honestly. "Where is the recording of me smoking whatever it is I'm holding? Hmm? Oh, you don't have it? That is a shame. As I have one myself... this is from the same night."

I turn DJ's laptop towards the table and put the recording of me and the girl outside.

Miranda turns ashen at the sight of me refusing the joint, and it's Ms. Pruitt who comments, adjusting her suit jacket, "Where is the proof that it's from the same party?"

"Both of us are wearing the same clothes as you can see... It's still winter. The owner of the house will confirm the security tapes' authenticity," I say, and she writes it down on her notepad while staring uncomfortably at her client. Ramsay, likewise, appears a bit less cocky than he was when he pranced in, loosening the collar of his polo shirt.

"Well, how do we know you didn't find some more drugs later?" Miranda is scrambling for a comeback. "Also, you mentioned in the first one that you did MDMA in the past! I don't think that is an environment for my daughter to grow up in!"

"Did I? Maybe I was just trying to impress a lady younger than me to assume I was cool." I smile without admitting to anything. "And interesting you should speak of the environment. Let's see a bit more about Tabitha's situation."

I put on a video from the luncheon, capturing exactly when she tells Tae off for having cake as they are both outside on the terrace, where the cameras captured the fight, and we observe my sibling running away crying.

Ramsay looks at his wife, slightly disgusted, and both attorneys exchange a glance.

I then hit 'play' on the recording from the brunch, where she grabs her arm, and my sister clearly cries out in pain and the people in the room here also gasp.

"You can't use that! I didn't agree to being filmed!" she yells, but her husband tells her off.

"Shut the fuck up Miranda, you just admitted the video is real, not what you told me the other day that his girl-friend fabricated it! What the hell!"

"As you all can see, I don't think it's my environment, which is the issue," I conclude the obvious. "I will also address your other accusation, that I would take illegal substances now with Tae with me. But first, I want to welcome some other guests..."

I send texts to DJ and her brother. The door to the left opens first, and my girlfriend comes in, followed by her ex.

"What the hell is going on?" Richard asks, looking around the room, but before anyone can answer, another door opens, and Marcus brings another man in, then backs away, shutting the door behind him.

"What the actual f...? Who are you, people? This isn't a tailor!" The young blond guy looks most confused of all of us then sees me. "Jon? What are you doing here? I was going to be fitted for a new suit!"

"Mm, you may be, but a different sort of outfit than you thought. How about you take a seat?" I point to a chair he quietly takes. Richard Simmons, however, isn't so amenable.

"DJ—why are Miranda and Ramsay here? You told me you had the 'Zephyr' for me! Why is your boyfriend here?"

"Oh, you mean the boyfriend you tried to blackmail me for. And the software I have been working on for years on? How about you shut the fuck up and sit down as well," Dahlia tells him, and I couldn't be happier by the look on his face. Well, I would if I could smash his face in.

"I didn't blackmail you! What are you talking about?" he tries to deny it, but by the way sweat gathers on his brow, he is worried.

"Maybe you should have checked if I didn't have a door-bell camera, you asshole," DJ laughs at him. "And a sign on the wall clearly informing you were being recorded! Here we go everyone—on how to be an idiot!"

She goes to the laptop, and we can all observe her ex showing up at her door. As they never left the hallway, we see and hear everything he tries to show her, including the obvious extortion attempt.

He now has at least the good sense to look contrite.

"McMaster, what is this shitshow?" Lexington intervenes and surprises me with his next comment. "I thought we are here to talk about Tabitha, not do a whole 'the butler did it' scene. I don't care about your girlfriend's little scuffle with her ex or your company's issues." His bushy eyebrows impatiently go up and down, and he runs his hand over his bald head.

"Well Lexington, you probably do care about the people your wife hires for the firm with your name on it, so this does affect you. But you are right, that wasn't just about Tae. It's also about clearing mine and DJ's names. That's why *he*—I point at the young blond guy who is making himself small—is in the room. Here is another video you may find interesting."

I put on the porch recording, where I refuse to smoke what the guy is offering, and everyone is silent at the end. Ramsay stares his wife down; Richard looks at the young man sitting in the corner with ire and nobody dares say a word. My lawyer is the one who speaks first.

"As you can see, my client not only didn't have any drugs on him. Unless this fellow deceived him, which by the way, is an offense punishable by a prison sentence. This shows Jon has a long-term commitment to his sister. Combined with the videos of Mrs. Lexington's behavior, it gives us sufficient cause to ask for full custody to be awarded to Mr. McMaster, and I am sure a judge will agree when we present our case. Jon and Tabitha are willing to allow Miranda and Ramsay to have the young lady over every other weekend, however, holiday arrangements can be made as well."

Ramsay just shakes his head, looking around the room. Miranda is trying to find something to say to the decisive points Eph made, but can't seem to articulate anything, just closes and opens her mouth a few times.

"Fine, McMaster," the older man in a golf outfit agrees in the end, "you made your point, and I am sorry about the predicament. Although I am not particularly close to Tabitha, she is a lovely girl and if she wants to stay with you, I can't in good conscience fight you, especially after the videos."

"But Ram!" his wife pleads with him, but he is having none of it.

"Shut up Miranda, look at the mess you made—and you!" He points at Richard. "You are fired! She may strut around being CEO, but I own that company and I don't need a blackmailing scum working for me!"

Richard's face is white now and tries to get up and leave.

"Why don't you wait a minute, Simmons," I say. "The fun is just about to begin! And Lexington, you may want to stay for this part as well. Our next guest is about to arrive!"

"What do you mean? Who is missing?" the billionaire asks.

The guy in the corner Marcus bought in earlier starts shifting uncomfortably, probably suspecting who else is coming.

DJ comments, ignoring the question, "Isn't it a bit weird how you all Big Men talk to each other using your surnames?"

"No, not really, just a Big Men thing," I answer playfully, in the 'groove' now. "Anyone wants something to drink? We got coffee and tea, just don't throw them at me," I inquire, looking at Miranda, who is whispering with her solicitor, still trying to get the upper hand. But by the look on Ms. Pruitt's face, she is as exasperated as we all are with the former model's antics.

We don't end up having any beverages as the doors open again and finally, Michaela enters the room typing on her phone, and we now have everyone in one place.

"Rich, I got your text and came as soon as I could. Luckily I was just around the corner with X-Access. Did you get the software? What the..." She freezes as looks up and sees eight pairs of eyes on her.

"Ah, glad you cut the bullshit and admitted straight off the bat that you know my ex-husband," Dahlia amuses herself. "Oh, and Richard, you may want to put a new password on that phone of yours." She throws him his mobile she accidentally 'found' when she walked him into the building.

"Umm yes, after you stole the code the other day, I reached out to Lex Aviation to work on the project jointly." Mike manages to turn the facts around with what I can see are years of expertise. And thinking back, I wonder how many times in the past 15 years she used these sorts of explanations on me.

"Joint project, is it? If I ask Miranda here, will she say the same thing?" I enquire, and I can only enjoy the anger in my stepmother's eyes as she glares at my ex-VP. "But now that you are here, let's do some introductions. The Lexingtons and our lawyers were here to discuss our custody arrangement for my sister before we go to an official hearing. Simmons, you know him well—he just lost his job trying to blackmail my girlfriend. You wouldn't happen to know anything about that, would you, Mike?"

"I know nothing of any blackmail," she grits her teeth.

"I am quite surprised you'd say so. Especially as I don't need to introduce you to our boy—Cole—here, right? Come on man, say hello to your... mother dearest."

There are gasps throughout the room, and interestingly, Miranda looks as shocked as everyone else. The young man has the good sense not to answer and cowers in his chair even more, as our guests stare between him and the silver-haired woman.

"Nothing to say? Bizarre how your son is in the same house when I get filmed in a less-than-ideal state. Lucky we can prove that I never took anything, and that I had no intention of doing so."

"There is no proof it was my son that recorded you. You have nothing to accuse us of. Everyone knows you took the boy under your wing, invited him to parties and all that."

"Perhaps, but a mighty coincidence, don't you think?" Dahlia asks, as in a well-rehearsed play. We may have rehearsed a bit, I admit. When we decided on a 'tell-all murder mystery' reveal, we had to prepare for some of their counters. "Even more interesting, how you held onto it up to now, as by itself, it clearly didn't stand on its own. No, you waited until Jon had something to fight for more than the company. The Board may frown at his playboy/party state, but it wouldn't have been enough to throw him out years ago. But now that you heard—probably from Richard—that Jon had a chance of getting custody, you gave it to my ex-husband to use to get my work. What we didn't understand up to recently is why? You had Jon thrown out, but we still had a contract for McAv to use it exclusively for years!"

"That is strange," Ramsay comments like he is part of the conversation. "Is it because my wife announced it, and Simmons needed to show something?"

"We also thought so at first," I begin the convoluted explanation. "But why would Mike care about your company? We are rivals in the end. As it turns out, she really doesn't. She does, however, care about money and power, and certain friendships she cultivated throughout the years."

DJ pulls up a series of emails we got from Anya. "As you can see, these are all from Michaela Jones's work email to a certain 'Mr. Smith' email account. So very innocent. But let's see some of the actual discussion. They really should have used a secure messaging app."

From: Michaela
To: Mr. Smith
We signed her. No code ownership, but will take whatever she puts on the server.
From: Mr. Smith
To: Michaela

Good start, get this done and we can talk government contract.

From: Michaela

To: Mr. Smith

He found the fax and Anya is out. Will have to check in myself.

From: Mr. Smith

To: Michaela

You do that, can't lose NASA

From: Michaela

To: Mr. Smith

Code is ready. Board is called for the afternoon; he will walk right into it. Send your son to Dahlia's house on Monday.

"As for the best part—someone here forgot to remove their signature from the bottom of their email..." DJ throws the last image and there is nowhere to hide now for Mike.

Kenneth Simmons

US Senator

The room is quiet again, and I put the finishing touches on the 'smoking gun'.

"After locating these emails, I called my good friend NASA Flight Director Gary Nichols—helps we are all Floridians—and turns out they did hear of the weather software. Because a certain senator assured them of ownership as part of a publicity stunt, whereas part of his re-election campaign he would be supporting space exploration, as it's all the trend these days with billionaires sending cars to the orbit, etc. But where it gets even more complicated is that... he heard of this software about a year and a half ago."

"Which is exactly when my ex-husband attempted to try to convince me to give our marriage another chance. When that failed, as he couldn't keep his dick in his pants, he convinced the judge to give him half the code," DJ fills them in, and the pieces of the puzzle all fitting together as she pulls extra pictures. "We also googled their names together after seeing the emails. Here, as you can see here in a picture from the Winter Ball in Los Angeles a couple of years back, the Senator is having an intense-looking conversation with... Ms. Jones."

"You fuckers, you played me!" Miranda explodes from her chair. "You never planned on giving me the software, did you?" she asks Richard, who doesn't answer.

"We don't think he ever did. They just needed a 'villain'—you, in case you were wondering—to convince me to work with someone they can access, in this case McAv," my girlfriend wraps it up. "I am sure that if it wasn't for that press conference and Mike's pushing, Jon wouldn't have allowed a contract without ownership, like you tried to have with me, and I refused. They were perhaps hoping I would just save everything on the company's servers, but it was mostly on my own company's private cloud."

DJ has a drink of water and continues. "They wanted to film me and my team probably while coding, and that is why Ms. Jones 'accidentally' let slip about my preference to work from home, which set Jon off and got me to come into the office. What they didn't anticipate, though, was me liking the IT department with its unpolished and dark ambiance instead of working upstairs in the very-camera-heavy but visually delightful main floors. That, and me disconnecting the cameras in there first chance I got."

"That little hitch also disturbed their fax-sending scheme to Lex Aviation, as they couldn't very well go by DJ's desk every day to send documents out," I add. "And I suspect our relationship—which randomly caused you to be in the office more than expected—was a bit of a surprise. Unfortunately, Mike found a way to use it, by having us sign the forms and show them to the Board exactly when the time was right for her. They put new cameras around your desk and got you on video as you came to make sure there were no accidental parts of the software saved locally in McAv's servers."

"That's enough!" Gus Lemkin, the Board member, is heard through the speakers. "We have all heard enough, and the evidence is quite compelling."

As Mike looks around the room in panic, DJ smiles. "Oh, we did forget to say we have been live streaming this to Jon's Board? We have a nice recording as well. It helps to have some reassurance that we won't find ourselves under an IRS audit sent by a certain member of the government as retribution for throwing a spanner in the works."

"McAv Aviation does not want to work with anyone using blackmail or this sort of manipulation, Ms. Jones. Consider yourself out of a job," the board representative continues. "Jon, I don't suppose you'd like your old post back?"

"You son of a bitch, you ruined everything," Michaela starts in a chilling voice. "I had it all worked out—I finally managed to get you out of my company. You should have never been given the CEO role, a tattooed playboy who never held a proper job in his life. It was my sweat and blood that kept McAv in business."

"Your father knew how good I was, how much I sacrificed," she continues quietly, staring into nothing, and the rest of people in the room stare at her like she lost the plot. "And then he passed away and you, golden boy, just get given the keys to MY kingdom. You, with your smiles and jokes with the staff, manage to convince them you can actually do the job. Sadly keeping it for so many years, while I do all the grunt work," Mike shakes her head in disbelief, as if all the effort I put in didn't matter.

"Grunt work? What the fuck are you talking about—you were VP handling contracts, not a janitor!" I counter, slightly shocked at her opinion.

"I should have been CEO. When Kenneth came to me with an offer to bring this stupid code, I jumped to the chance to get some proper government connections for his help. You just had to go and sleep with her, didn't you, and mess everything up?"

"You messed everything up, and now everybody knows exactly what you are. Using your son, Richard, Anya and even Miranda here just to get to a job which my father would have never given you, despite your delusions of grandeur." I get up myself, towering over her. "You know why? Because you can manage contracts and handle admin tasks, but without me to charm everyone, and to have actual on-the-job conversations with the engineers and technicians, you would have run McAv into the ground.

Oh, and the police want to talk to you as well. You won't be getting away with only losing your job and a pat on the back."

I look towards the cameras instead of Mike, who no longer interests me.

"Lemkin, my name is on the fucking company headers. I should have never been kicked out. When I'm back, I will be revising my contract in detail. Especially as my mate Gary from NASA would certainly like to collaborate with Dahlia and myself—and by extension McAv—on using and testing the weather predictor. Guess that would really be a good selling point for us, don't you agree?"

"What? A NASA contract? That would be fantastic. Our customers will buy everything we offer if we are part of the space race!" Another board member pitches in, but I can't tell who it is by just the voice. "McMaster, that is great news! Let's meet in the office next week!"

"Yeah let's. But for now—anyone else here has anything to say? No? In that case, I'll show you all the exit. Hey Lexington—maybe we can talk about reducing some costs if both our companies are in the same state."

"Thank wouldn't be a bad shout actually," Ramsay agrees as he takes his fuming wife by the elbow and walks her out, followed by Richard and Cole. In the end, Michaela retreats, looking at me with years of hatred in her eyes. The lawyers are last to leave as they continue to talk about the paperwork they each need to file for Tabitha's custody.

I finally collapse in a chair and put my forehead on the table, as I can't believe it's truly done. I got Tae and my company back. And I don't have to worry about any more backstabbers or blackmailers.

When I feel arms around me, I smile as the coconut and vanilla scent surrounds me and reminds me that I gained far more than just McAv and my sister. I won a smart and incredibly sexy warrior who stood by me today, and hopefully will stick around.

"Hey Avril." I get up and turn towards her and sit her down in my lap. "Guess we prevailed," I summarize, and I see her roll her eyes at my fancy word use.

"Yes Poirot, we took the prize in this 'whodunit' we orchestrated, all was missing was you playing with your mustache." She grins at me and runs her fingers through my beard, luckily my facial hair not long enough for the famed detective's twirl. "You should get a gold star for you for spotting an opportunity with Miranda's husband."

"I saw today he was actually a reasonable guy, despite his reputation of being a ruthless businessman. I never had that long a conversation with him before, and I hope we can have a good business relationship. But I think I had enough of CEOs, exes, and lawyers. You want to go home?"

"Hell yes, let's go home!" DJ says the words I want to hear from her. Without further talking, I just get off the chair still holding her, then put her over my shoulder in her favorite—yet unconfessed—position to be taken home in. Over the sound of her laughter, I take my woman to my car.

DJ — THREE MONTHS LATER

A hand gently climbs up my thigh, driving the sheet off me, and the warmth of my man encompasses me, is touching my back, as I am completely naked and basking in his heat. His stiff dick is pushing against my ass, and he moves my hair out of the way so he can kiss my neck and shoulder. His palm moves up, cupping my breast, rubbing me, and my nipples harden against his fingers.

Obviously satisfied, Jon gives my bud one final pinch, causing me to gasp, then his digits travel to his favorite place, opening my folds and massaging my clit in an up-and-down motion, getting me ready for him. I turn my head and he captures my lips in a heart-stopping kiss, his tongue invading my mouth, conquering me, just as he breaches his pussy with two of his fingers, slowly pumping in and out.

I moan against him, the dual sensations maddening, and he mumbles, "Avril, what you do to me," before lifting my leg and lining his erection to my entrance.

"How do you want it, love, fast and light or hard and deep?" he asks like he doesn't know the answer already.

"All of it, just fuck me, Jon!" I beg, and he grabs my tits again as he delves inside slowly. He then starts moving in the short bursts the position allows, all the while ravaging my mouth with deep advances of his tongue.

"Yeah, take me, I need you to take all of me," he says before changing the ballgame, flipping me on my front and lifting my ass in the air.

He pauses for a moment, running his fingers up and down my slit, and I have never felt so worshiped, as he licks me from behind, burrowing his tongue in my channel, sucking me and making me even wetter. I push against his face, trying to get more and more friction, but what I get is a smack, as I feel his large palm marking my ass.

"Now, now, greedy girl, you have to wait for me to plea-sure you." He chuckles and I turn my head, giving him a death glare, which makes his dimple pop even more. "But if you insist..." He shoves his throbbing thick cock in one thrust, then starts using me like I want it. He punishes my pussy with his movements, his fingers grab my hips to push himself in even harder, and the grunts I hear from him only match my wails. He only stops to spread my ass cheeks open and uses some of my slick to press his thumb against my other hole, as he knows damn well that drives me insane.

"Oh Avril, I want that ass again tonight, to feel you so tight around me, as I put that dildo in your pussy and pound you all night long." His breaths grow shallower and shallower as he pumps both his dick and finger in my openings, and with every advance and retreat I start shaking, chasing my climax, ready to fall off for him, to shatter for him.

"Fuck Jon, just like that!" I cry, and as he grants my wish as I feel his thighs hitting my ass time and time again, his manhood owning me and I come with a scream, pulsating around him, as he releases deep in my cunt with a manly growl, before crashing on top of me, wrecked by his own orgasm.

"I know I don't tell you enough, but—I love you Dahlia," he whispers in my ear as he squishes me with all his weight and lays over me.

"I love you too Jon, but I'd love you even more if I could breathe." I try to laugh but I have a literal bear on me.

"Har, har." He pokes me in the ribs as he rolls over me but pulls me to him and kisses my forehead. "I can't believe we are here."

"Umm, you better believe it. We both signed the sale contract, caveman. It's ours now." I wave my hand at our new bedroom, in our recently bought villa by the beach.

It has more of a Spanish style than the classic Miami-white vibe, but we love the access to the ocean and the many balconies and terraces. We even found one with a deck by the kitchen so Jon can read his fantasy e-books and discover more ridiculously swanky words to use in daily speech. Tae has her own wing, so she doesn't have to...

'listen to us go at it' which I agree is an advantage. Jon doesn't realize the 'advantage' will soon go both ways, but I won't be enlightening him just yet.

Over six weeks ago, as we were finally ready to fly the Cessna, my boyfriend put a business card next to my toolkit and casually—too casually, as I was not paying attention to him while testing the propeller—mentioned.

"Here DJ, just in case you feel like moving in with us officially, my estate agent has a few houses for us to see."

It didn't register with me initially, but then I looked over at the card and then at him; and then at the card again; and then at Jon again, who by now was grinning like a fool.

"Is this how you ask me if I want to move in with you? For real? You really are an idiot!" I laughed at him, then jumped in his arms, kissing his stupid face. He laughed as well, putting me down to avoid triggering the techs in the hangar to start clapping.

"So that's a 'yes' then? Do I have the honor of officially getting hit by your erratic limbs every night?"

"Very funny caveman. Just for that, I may try to cook something!" I countered, still enjoying the feel of his embrace.

"Lovely. I'll make sure all the rooms have working fire alarms as a priority, then." He shook his head, knowing damn well I was not about to even start the stove.

"You better! Oh and offices for both of us, can't share with you and your OCD-ways!"

"Yeah Avril, we will buy a giant McMansion so you can have your messy workplace and I can have one where I can actually see the desk without all the papers and computer parts. Lucky that NASA contract got us all a ton of money."

Not that either of us were struggling before, but the 'Zephyr' software sales were amazing, not just with the Space agency but also with some of the Big named airlines after I relented and allowed Jon to franchise it early.

Jon also opened the other files Anya sent, and as to his surprise, she did a thorough audit of all McAv departments, identifying weaknesses—for example the layout of the seat assembly line adding about half an hour of unnecessary back and forth by the fitters or some comments on glaring legal loopholes in employment contracts. The changes we implemented after that also contributed to a very pleasing-to-the-Board profit increase.

So we were now in our new house, and unfortunately, had to get out of bed and prepare for our housewarming party.

"I don't suppose your sister can hold the event by herself seeing as she was the one who organized it for us." Jon sighs, holding me tighter. "I could just spend all day here with you."

"Well, I am sure she could, but as we have about 30 people coming, some may wonder where we are... you know, as hosts and all. Fair warning, Laura will probably come find us."

"Uh, indeed, she has no boundaries, does she?"

"No, she doesn't... suspect we will have some fun later with her running into your Nate."

"Oh, dear," Jon grunts, "it's going to be like having an unexploded grenade meeting a terrier."

"They'll be just fine. Luckily, they won't jump each other's bones, with him not going for women with kids and her not interested in men she can see more than one night. Come on then, let's get that booze out. We are going to need it," I say, and drag my man after me in the bathroom to clean up, before setting down to welcome our guests.

"Come along, Jon, we have to go!"

"Why? It's not like they will burn the place down!"

And those are what one would call... famous last words.

Thank you, dear reader, for sticking with this novel until the very end.

If you had a blast and want more, my next book, "Gambling with the Player", Laura and Nate's story, is expected to be published in March 2023 with pre-orders available in January.

The last installment in the trilogy, featuring Anya and Marcus, is targeting a release in June 2023. I know a few of you want to know more about what is driving Anya to do the things she did in this book.

ACKNOWLEDGMENTS

Many thanks to my husband for bearing with me while I discovered writing and Tiktok videos.

And to my beta readers especially Karen who gave me a great idea or two.

Also, Google-you rock, I am not that witty without you.

For more, please visit my website mirelaholtauthor.com and sign-up to my newsletter or follow me on my various social media sites

Facebook: mirelaholtauthor

TikTok: @mirelaholtauthor

Instagram: mirelaholtauthor

I don't have the patience to do more social media, sorry.

Printed in Great Britain
by Amazon